THE NEW HEBREW THROUGH PRAYER

1

Roberta Osser Baum

Consultants:
Rabbi Martin Cohen
Rabbi William Cutter

BEHRMAN HOUSE, INC.

Book and Cover Design: Irving S. Berman
Electronic Composition and Page Production:
21st Century Publishing and Communications, Inc.
Special Needs Education Consultant:
Sara Rubinow Simon

CONTENTS

I. INTRODUCTION AND OVERVIEW

PREFACE

You are about to embark on a sacred task, the task of teaching our children how to worship, to pray in the Hebrew language. In doing so, you will help them connect with our God, with our ancestors, and with our heritage.

As Jewish educators, we want to help our students develop positive attitudes toward our rich Jewish tradition. Toward this end, *Hineni—The New Hebrew Through Prayer* is designed to deepen our students' understanding of Jewish ritual and the concepts inherent in our mitzvot, while teaching them to read Hebrew and to pray. The prayer selections introducing each lesson encourage participation in the rituals of synagogue and home. And the enrichment activities aid students in developing reading fluency, allowing for active participation in the classroom setting. This approach encourages students to feel comfortable in their learning environment, where they sharpen their reading skills and develop a familiarity and understanding of ritual and mitzvot.

USING THIS TEACHER'S EDITION

This Teacher's Edition contains the entire text of *Hineni— The New Hebrew Through Prayer 1*, reproduced in reduced size. The pages are annotated with suggested activities, teaching methods, and other information to assist you. Black-line masters that supplement the material are also provided in this Teacher's Edition.

Keep in mind that students learn in different ways, and any student's primary learning mode may be aural, visual, or tactile. Similarly, teachers teach in different ways. Don't feel obligated to use a method that does not feel comfortable with your teaching style. By the same token, remember that since students learn in different ways, you should vary your teaching methods accordingly. Feel free to repeat an activity or method that worked especially well for you and your students.

> The information and suggestions in this Teacher's Edition are intended to assist you in developing your own teaching plan. You do not need to follow every suggestion on every page. Rather, the guide provides you with many different options from which to choose.

Pacing

Students differ in ability. Teachers differ in style. Schools differ in the number of class sessions scheduled each week. Ultimately, you must decide how to pace your class through the text.

The lessons in *Hineni* vary in length. Some lessons may take three or more sessions, while others will take one or two. A short but more difficult lesson may take more time to teach than a longer, simpler lesson.

Homework

Whether or not to give homework is a question that should be addressed to your school principal. Keep in mind that homework can provide students with the additional contact, repetition, and reinforcement of what has already been learned in class. Homework should not be used as a tool to teach new information.

If you do give homework, *Hineni* makes assigning homework easy. At the end of each lesson in the Teacher's Edition is a review worksheet. These review worksheets can be duplicated and completed for homework, or, of course, they can be used for in-class evaluation.

Be sure to review each homework assignment during the class session following the assignment. Doing this reinforces the importance of the homework and reassures the students that their efforts were noted and were a worthwhile expenditure of time.

Family Education

A partnership between home and school can help your students reach their greatest potential in their Hebrew studies. Parents can be important allies in the education of your students, and every effort should be made to facilitate this partnership. To aid you in this endeavor, black-line masters to duplicate and send home for the family are included in this Teacher's Edition.

OVERVIEW OF LESSON PLANNING

Timing is an important factor in planning your classes. Keep in mind the objectives of the program as you plan your lesson for the day. Foremost in your mind should be not how quickly you move through the text, but rather how effectively you teach the material and how thoroughly the students master it. Remember that review and reinforcement are essential ingredients for mastery.

There are nine lessons in *Hineni 1*. How you pace your class should depend on the number of classroom sessions each week, your students' reading ability, and the length of the particular passages. It is important to decide beforehand which activities you will cover in each session and how much time you will allot to each activity. Make sure that reading is a part of *every* lesson. The materials in the textbook and in this Teacher's Edition, as well as teacher reinforcement through games and Word Card work, should all come into play to ensure the success of the program.

REINFORCING PRAYER AWARENESS

Developing comfort and familiarity with the prayers on the part of your students is an important aspect of your goal. Several strategies can help you to achieve this objective.

Prayer Service

Begin each class with a short (two- to five-minute) prayer service, including the prayers learned to date. Ask individual students to take turns as leaders.

You may choose to end the service by having the class recite this blessing.

בָּרוּךְ אַתָּה, יְיָ אֱלֹהֵינוּ, מֶלֶךְ הָעוֹלָם, אֲשֶׁר קִדְּשָׁנוּ בְּמִצְוֹתָיו וְצִוָּנוּ לַעֲסוֹק בְּדִבְרֵי תוֹרָה.

Praised are You, Adonai our God, Ruler of the world, who makes us holy with commandments and commands us to be involved with the words of Torah.

Create Your Own Prayerbook

After learning each prayer, you may ask students to write the prayer and its English meaning in a personal prayerbook. Students may wish to write the prayers in calligraphy (see below) and illustrate or illuminate their work. These prayerbooks can then be used at every class prayer service.

Calligraphy

Most lessons offer an opportunity for students to practice Hebrew calligraphy. This can be done on a variety of levels: simple printing, copying a text, or learning formal calligraphy as practiced by a *sofer* (scribe).

Students can use any writing medium, but we recommend investing in felt-tip pens specifically designed for calligraphy. They are inexpensive, and the results justify the expenditure.

You may wish to exhibit students' efforts on bulletin boards and in other displays.

TEACHING AIDS
Chalkboard

Use the chalkboard to introduce new words and prayers, to answer questions, to play games, and to present assignments.

Remember to vary the way in which you use the chalkboard. This can be as simple as changing the chalk color or varying the size of the letters you write.

Draw a picture on the chalkboard to illustrate the lesson. (The less polished an artist you are, the more the class will love your drawings.)

Incorporate children's need for physical movement. Plan quick-paced exercises that involve coming to the board. For example, have students copy a word that you have written on the board. There is really nothing more special about writing on a chalkboard than on paper—unless you are a child. Coming to the front of the room and writing on the board is exciting to many students. If they enjoy using the board, let them do so.

Flannelboard

A flannelboard can be used with the entire class, with small groups, or by a single student. It saves writing time at the chalkboard and presents letters and words exactly as they appear in a printed book. It also offers students the opportunity to manipulate words to form whole phrases.

Flannelboards can be purchased at a school supplies store or may be easily constructed by covering a large piece of cardboard with flannel. You can make flannelboard words by gluing a small piece of velcro or sandpaper onto the back of existing Word Cards or by cutting flashcards out of rough-textured construction paper. Most flannelboard techniques will also work with a magnetic board.

The flannelboard can be used to introduce new words and display them clearly. It is also useful for drill or review.

DEVELOPING READING SKILLS

Alef Bet Review

Begin the year with a thorough review of the letters and vowels in the Hebrew alphabet. Use an *alef-bet* poster, *alef-bet* flashcards, or the Word Cards for the students' primer from the previous year. You can also use a transitional reading text such as the *Back-to-School Hebrew Reading Refresher* to review and drill Hebrew decoding before students begin *Hineni*.

Stopwatch and Tape Recorder

A stopwatch is an easy way to assess improvement in reading fluency. It can be used to time the speed at which a student reads a passage. Many students enjoy the experience of competing against and trying to improve their own best time.

A tape recorder also provides students with tangible evidence of their improvement. Record members of the class as they read a passage. Remember the order in which they have read. Two or three weeks later, record the students, in the same order, while they read the passage on a second tape, then play back both and compare.

Word Cards

There is a set of Word Cards available for use with *Hineni 1*. These cards, printed on durable, heavy cardboard, include all key words covered by the book. (Each Word Card is numbered for easy reference to activities included in this Teacher's Edition.) The English meaning is on the back of each Word Card.

Word Cards may be used by individuals or small groups of students, or by the class as a whole. Activities should be both teacher and student initiated, to reinforce reading skills. Possible games and teaching strategies using Word Cards are endless, and each teacher will develop many ways of using them. The following suggestions may be implemented as presented here or adapted as necessary.

Remember to use the Word Cards regularly and with a variety of techniques.

General Word Card Techniques and Games

1. Display a number of Words Cards on the edge of the chalkboard or in a pocket chart. Provide a clue about one of the words and ask the students to read the correct word. For example, "This is the Jewish state"—*Yisrael*.

2. Distribute Word Cards to the class. Call out, one at a time, the Hebrew words and phrases found on the individual cards. Ask the student with the matching card to supply the correct answer by standing up, displaying the card, and reading the word or phrase.

3. Make a packet of ten Word Cards. Arrange the class in a circle (sitting or standing) and have the students pass the packet around the circle while playing music on a tape or CD player. (Try to use Jewish or Israeli music.) When the music stops, the student holding the packet should read and/or translate the top card. This card is then placed at the bottom of the pile and the game continues in the same fashion.

4. Create two rows of Word Cards with six cards in each row. Ask students individually (or in two teams) to choose a row. Taking turns, ask the individual students or teams to read the six Hebrew words, then switch and read the words in the other row. You can also play the game by translating the words instead of reading them.

5. Post at least six words in a column on the board. Ask individuals or teams to take turns "climbing up the ladder" by reading and translating the words in the column in ascending order. Score one point for each word read correctly and two points for each word translated correctly. Then play again by having students read the words in descending order to climb down the ladder.

6. Place Word Cards on the edge of the chalkboard in full view of the class. Read the words one at a time, calling on students to go to the board and remove the identified card. Variation: Have one of the students read the words.

7. You can play a memory game with double sets of Word Cards (two identical cards for each word). Lay out eight pairs of words (sixteen cards in all) upside down and shuffled, in rows. Call on a student to pick a card and read it aloud, then try to find its match. If successful, the student must then tell the meaning of the word in order to keep the pair. On successfully giving the meaning, the student keeps the cards and two new cards are put down. If the student is unsuccessful, then the initial cards are returned to their place face down. Then the next student goes.

Pronunciation and Translation

1.   Show a card and ask for volunteers to read.

2.   Show a card and read together with the class.

3.   Lightning Review: Show a card to one student, who has 5–10 seconds to pronounce the word; immediately show the next card to another student until everyone has participated.

4.   Ask students to drill each other.

Reinforcing Word Order

1. Place cards on a flannelboard in the correct order; have students read the prayer (as a group and individually).

2. Ask students to close their eyes; remove one or more cards. Ask which words are missing.

3. Scramble all the cards for the words in a prayer. Ask students to place the cards in the correct order.

4. Scramble all the cards for the words in a prayer and put one or more aside. Ask students to place cards in the correct order and determine what is missing.

5. Distribute all the cards in a prayer, one per student. Ask students to come to the front of the room and stand in the order of the words of the prayer.

6. Distribute all the cards in a prayer, one per student, plus extra words not from the prayer. Proceed as in step 5 above, but ask students holding the extra words to step aside.

Word Cards

The following is a list of words included in *Hineni 1*:

the world	הָעוֹלָם	.37	praise!	בָּרְכוּ	.1
who	אֲשֶׁר	.38	Adonai	יְיָ	.2
makes us holy	קִדְּשָׁנוּ	.39	who is to be praised	הַמְבֹרָךְ	.3
with God's commandments	בְּמִצְוֹתָיו	.40	praised, blessed	בָּרוּךְ	.4
and commands us	וְצִוָּנוּ	.41	forever and ever	לְעוֹלָם וָעֶד	.5
to light	לְהַדְלִיק	.42	brings on the evening	מַעֲרִיב עֲרָבִים	.6
a light, candle	נֵר	.43	living, lives	חַי	.7
of	שֶׁל	.44	and eternal	וְקַיָּם	.8
Shabbat	שַׁבָּת	.45	will rule	יִמְלֹךְ	.9
who creates	בּוֹרֵא	.46	forms	יוֹצֵר	.10
(the) fruit (of)	פְּרִי	.47	light	אוֹר	.11
the vine	הַגֶּפֶן	.48	and creates	וּבוֹרֵא	.12
who brings forth	הַמּוֹצִיא	.49	darkness	חֹשֶׁךְ	.13
bread	לֶחֶם	.50	makes	עֹשֶׂה	.14
from	מִן	.51	peace	שָׁלוֹם	.15
the earth	הָאָרֶץ	.52	all things, everything	הַכֹּל	.16
tree	עֵץ	.53	hear	שְׁמַע	.17
shofar	שׁוֹפָר	.54	Israel	יִשְׂרָאֵל	.18
in the sukkah	בַּסֻּכָּה	.55	our God	אֱלֹהֵינוּ	.19
lulav	לוּלָב	.56	one	אֶחָד	.20
Ḥanukkah	חֲנֻכָּה	.57	name	שֵׁם	.21
miracles	נִסִּים	.58	glory of	כְּבוֹד	.22
at this season, at this time	בַּזְּמַן הַזֶּה	.59	God's kingdom	מַלְכוּתוֹ	.23
who has given us life	שֶׁהֶחֱיָנוּ	.60	you shall love	וְאָהַבְתָּ	.24
the earth	הָאֲדָמָה	.61	your heart	לְבָבְךָ	.25
eating (of)	אֲכִילַת	.62	the words	הַדְּבָרִים	.26
matzah	מַצָּה	.63	as a sign	לְאוֹת	.27
maror, bitter herbs	מָרוֹר	.64	mezuzot	מְזֻזוֹת	.28
sanctification	קִדּוּשׁ	.65	your house	בֵּיתֶךָ	.29
memory	זִכָּרוֹן	.66	who	מִי	.30
work of creation	(לְ)מַעֲשֵׂה בְרֵאשִׁית	.67	like You	כָּמֹכָה, כָּמְכָה	.31
memory	זֵכֶר	.68	among the gods (other nations worship)	בָּאֵלִם	.32
going out from Egypt	(לִ)יצִיאַת מִצְרָיִם	.69	majestic	נֶאְדָּר	.33
in (with) love	בְּאַהֲבָה	.70	in (the) holiness	בַּקֹּדֶשׁ	.34
and in (with) favor	וּבְרָצוֹן	.71	you	אַתָּה	.35
			ruler	מֶלֶךְ	.36

CLASSROOM GAMES

Games can add variety and interest to a lesson. They reinforce learning through a medium that quickly catches the students' attention. As you plan to use the games found below, or others you develop on your own, keep the following considerations in mind:

1. Use games that move quickly.

2. Stop when students' interest begins to lag.

3. Choose games appropriate to the age group.

4. When playing a game with the entire class, see that all students become actively involved.

5. Choose games that contribute to improving specific skills and reading fluency.

6. Use games that are easy to follow and organize. Explain rules clearly. Avoid complicated directions. You want students' attention focused on the skills being reinforced, not on rules.

7. Maintain control of the class.

What's Missing?

Decide on a set of lines in a prayer passage from which to draw words. Divide the class into two teams, then choose a word and write it without vowels in two different places on the chalkboard. Each team (with members playing individually, one at a time, or as a group) must locate the word in the set of lines, go to the board and, using the book for reference, add the vowels. The first team to do so then gets the chance to read the word correctly (from either the board or the book), and if correct, they score a point. If incorrect, then the other team (having located the word and written in the vowels) gets a chance to read and score a point.

Word Search

This game will help students recognize phrases within a prayer passage. Each student has a pencil, paper, and text open to a prayer passage. (The teacher might choose to focus the students' attention on a given set of lines within the passage.) The class is divided into two teams. The teacher reads a word aloud. Students search for the word and write it down, along with the word immediately following it, to complete a phrase.

(A word is often found more than once in a prayer passage; therefore, more than one answer is possible.) Students are given a specified amount of time to search for the word and write the phrase. The teacher calls "Stop" and pencils are put down. A point is given for each team member who found and wrote the phrase in the allotted time.

Variation: Instead of writing the phrase, the teacher calls out the first word in a phrase, then the two team players search for the word and race to the chalkboard (or any other "target"). The first to hit the "target" reads the phrase and earns a point for the team.

Speed Reading
Individual Competition

Using a watch with a second hand, or a stopwatch, time individual students reading an assigned set of lines three separate times. The goal is for the students to improve their previous record. If the student reads a word incorrectly, ask the student to repeat the word correctly in order to proceed. Allow each student a maximum time of 60 seconds before proceeding to the next student. You may also allow students their own choice of lines to read.

Teams

Divide the class into two teams—Team A and Team B. Select a prayer passage (or set of lines) for students to read. Ask each student on Team A to read a word or line in turn until the passage is completed, while timing the team. Then ask Team B to try to achieve a better time while reading the same selection in the same manner. Then reverse, using a different prayer passage or set of lines, with Team B going first. If a reader makes a mistake, ask him or her to read the word correctly before proceeding. (Alternative: When a word is read incorrectly, the word should be "passed along" to the next student who finishes the first student's word[s] and then continues with his or her own.)

Class

Announce a target time—a period of time for the class to beat while reading a particular prayer passage or set of lines. Ask each student to read one word in turn. If the class beats the target time, ask them to repeat the activity and try to beat the new time.

Tic-Tac-Toe

Draw a Tic-Tac-Toe diagram on the chalkboard. Divide students into two teams, X and O. Show a Word Card, then call on a student from Team X to read the Hebrew word. If the student reads correctly, ask him or her to place an X in one of the squares. Then it is Team O's turn; show another Word Card, and call on a student from Team O to read it.

Variations:

- Students must read the word on the Word Card and read the sentence (or line) in the prayer passage that contains the word before placing a mark in a square. (You can facilitate the game by telling the student which line contains the word.)

- Students must read the Hebrew and give the English meaning before placing an X or an O in a square.

- Students must answer questions about the prayer passage(s) in order to place an X or an O in a square.

- After drawing the Tic-Tac-Toe diagram, write the names of the prayer passages in the squares. Ask each student to choose a square and read the name of the prayer correctly in order to place an X or O in the square.

Beat the Clock

Draw the face of a clock on the chalkboard, but do *not* write the numbers. Draw the hands at the position of 12 o'clock. Think of a word that appears in one of the prayer passages (or ask a student to think of one) and draw horizontal lines on the board—one for each letter in the word. The lines should be next to each other. Then call on individual students to guess which letters are contained in the word. When a student guesses a letter correctly, write that letter over the line that corresponds to the place in the word where the letter appears. If the letter appears more than once, write it on multiple lines. If the student guesses a letter that is not in the word, then add an hour to the face of the clock on the chalkboard; first draw the 1, then the 2, the 3, etc. The object of the game is to guess the word before the clock "strikes 12."

Concentration

Place cards with Hebrew words and cards with the English translations in random order in a pocket chart or on the bottom edge of the chalkboard. Number the backs of the Hebrew words with even numbers and the English words with odd numbers. Then turn the cards over so only the numbers are showing. Ask students individually (or in teams) to try to match the Hebrew and English word pairs by calling out two numbers, one even (for the Hebrew) and one odd (for the English). Turn the two cards over. If they match, then

the player scores a point and the matched pair of cards is removed. If they do not match, place the cards back in their original position and ask another student, or the other team, to go. The game continues until all sets have been matched and removed. The player or team with more sets of cards wins.

Hebrew Baseball

Divide the class into two teams. On the board, draw a baseball diamond and a score board. Appoint a student to keep score. Determine the number of words that must be read successfully in order for the reader to earn a "single," "double," "triple," and "home run." Then, as students on each team come "to bat," they can individually decide how many bases to try for—in order to get on base they must then read correctly that number of words from a prayer passage assigned by you. If a student reads incorrectly, he or she is "out" and the next team member goes. After three outs, change teams and repeat. Play for as many innings as you like.

Stop!

This reading game may be used for oral reading practice, review of English meanings, or recognition of prefixes, suffixes, and roots. Assign a student to read until a specific word is reached (for example, instruct the class: "Please read until you come to the Hebrew word for 'ruler.'"). Ask the class to call out "Stop!" when the reader reaches the designated word. Then continue with other students. This game may be played individually or in teams.

Hebrew Bingo

Select 16 Hebrew words or phrases. Prepare a Bingo board with 16 squares. In ten of the squares, chosen at random, write Hebrew words or phrases from among the 16 you selected, leaving the other six squares blank. On a separate piece of paper, draw six boxes (the same size as those on the Bingo board) and write in the remaining six Hebrew words or phrases. Call this card the Extra Word card.

Duplicate enough copies of both the Bingo board and the Extra Word card for every student in your class. Then, have your students cut up the six word boxes on the Extra Word card and paste or tape them at random in the empty boxes on the Bingo board. When the Bingo boards are ready, give each student small objects to use as markers. (The markers can be paper clips, pennies, or any other similar item.) To play, you should call out one of the 16 Hebrew words or phrases for the students to find and cover. The first student to cover four squares in a row (horizontally, vertically, or diagonally), and then read the covered words correctly, wins.

Variation: Instead of reading the 16 Hebrew words and phrases yourself, cut up one set of the words and phrases into individual words and phrases and place them in a container. Go around the class asking students individually

Jeopardy

Create categories by (a) selecting Word Cards and (b) designing 3 x 5 Question Cards about prayers, blessings, rituals, values, etc. The first and easiest item in each category is worth 5 points. As point values increase, the Word Cards and Question Cards progress in difficulty. Write the number of points on the back of each card. Place cards in a pocket chart or on a bulletin board, with the backs facing the students. Label each category.

Divide the class into two or more teams. The first player chooses a category and the degree of difficulty, i.e., the number of points. If the player reads the Word Card correctly or answers the Question Card correctly, the team receives the number of points on the back of the card. The card is then removed from play. If the player's response is incorrect, the card remains in the game and is returned to its original position. Teams alternate. The game continues until all cards have been removed. The team with the most points wins the game.

Siddur Squares

This is a game for the whole class. It can be played using the questions from one of the lessons, or as a review of several lessons.

Select nine students to serve as the "siddur squares." (You might place nine chairs in a Tic-Tac-Toe board arrangement.) Divide the remaining students into two teams, X and O. You or a student can serve as moderator.

The first player on Team X will select one of the nine siddur squares, and the moderator will ask one of the prepared questions from the lesson being reviewed. The siddur square student should give an answer, and the Team X player must agree or disagree with the answer. If the Team X player is correct (that is, agrees with a correct answer or disagrees with an incorrect answer), then Team X should receive an X in that square. You may wish to draw a Tic-Tac-Toe board on the chalkboard to facilitate score keeping.

Continue in the same fashion with Team O. Continue, alternating teams, until one team has three squares in a row, diagonally, vertically, or horizontally.

Matching Questions with Answers

Write questions about the prayer passages on colored paper and put them in a box. Write answers to the questions on white paper and put them in a second box. Divide the class into Team A and Team B. Ask each student on Team A to take a question from the question box, and each student on Team B to take an answer from the answer box. Ask a player from Team A to read his or her question, and ask a student from Team B who thinks his or her card has the correct answer to read the card. Continue this way, asking another Team A member to read a question, and Team B to try to find the correct answer. After all the questions and answers have been correctly matched, collect and return them to their respective boxes and reverse the assignments so that members of Team B have the questions, and Team A the answers.

II. USING THE TEXTBOOK

INTRODUCING THE TEXTBOOK

Draw students' attention to the title of the book, "הִנֵּנִי."

Explain:

הִנֵּנִי means "Here I am" (הִנֵּה אֲנִי). The deep significance of the reply, הִנֵּנִי, is apparent from the first time it is used in the Torah. Abraham was the first person to answer הִנֵּנִי when God called upon him. His answer indicated his readiness to serve God (Genesis 22:1–3).

Generations later, God called to Moses from the burning bush. Again, the answer was הִנֵּנִי (Exodus 3:1–4), and Moses served God by leading the Children of Israel out of Egypt.

And yet generations later, Samuel expressed his readiness to serve God as a prophet when he said הִנֵּנִי (I Samuel 3).

The reply הִנֵּנִי indicates a readiness to listen and to serve God through action. You have heard your name and understand it to be a personal call. When we say הִנֵּנִי today, we indicate a willingness to step forward and continue in the tradition of our ancestors. With our faith in God, with God's faith in our abilities, and with assistance from others, we are ready to accomplish all that is before us.

LEARNING OBJECTIVES

Prayer Reading Skills

Family letters: בּ ב כּ כ ך

Root: ב ר כ ("bless," "praise")

Final letter review

First Torah blessing

Prayer Concepts

God's name: Adonai

The significance of reciting the בָּרְכוּ

- as the Call to Prayer
- as the introduction to the blessing said before reading from the Torah

BEYOND THE TEXTBOOK

The *dagesh*: the dot in the middle of a letter

Reading: כָּל כָל ("oh" or "aw")

"Eye" ending (אָי אַי)

Alef bet review

Term: מִנְיָן

ABOUT THE PRAYER

The בָּרְכוּ is the official Call to Prayer in the morning and evening services. It summons the community—the congregation—to join together in prayer. Since the *minyan* represents the community as a whole, this ancient prayer is traditionally recited only when a *minyan* is present.

INSTRUCTIONAL MATERIALS

Textbook pages 4–13

Word Cards 1–5

Worksheet for Lesson 1

Family Education: "As a Family: Coming Together in Community" (at the back of this guide)

SET INDUCTION

Coming Together

Discuss with your students how they know when it is time for the class to begin.

- What did they do before coming together that set the tone for the class? *(brought Hebrew and Judaic textbooks from home; perhaps put on* kippot *when they entered the building or classroom; passed by Jewish symbols such as a mezuzah or* tallit *or Star of David on the way to class)*

- What signal is used by your school, or by you, to call everyone together for the start of class? *(ring a bell; flicker the lights; greet the class; give verbal instructions; close the classroom door)*

- Why do we come together as one class, instead of remaining as individuals, each doing our own thing and learning on our own? *(we learn from each other; we enjoy being together; we form a community of teacher and students)*

Visualizing the Concept

Draw a circle on the chalkboard, then draw lines radiating out from the circle (like a sun), one line for each student in the class. Write the students' names, one per line. Now write the name of your religious school and the grade of your class in the center of the circle. (*"Temple _____," and "כִּתָּה ב" or "Fourth Grade"*) Tell your students that this is a diagram of your class community.

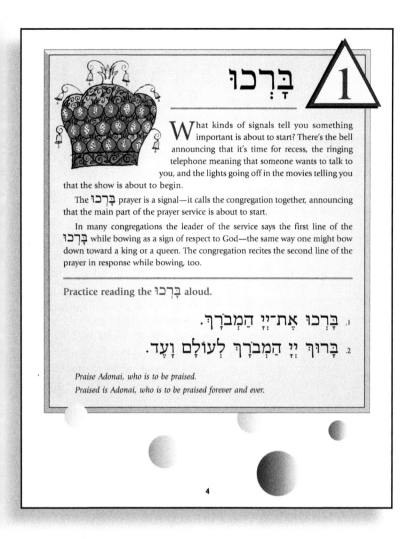

בָּרְכוּ

1

What kinds of signals tell you something important is about to start? There's the bell announcing that it's time for recess, the ringing telephone meaning that someone wants to talk to you, and the lights going off in the movies telling you that the show is about to begin.

The בָּרְכוּ prayer is a signal—it calls the congregation together, announcing that the main part of the prayer service is about to start.

In many congregations the leader of the service says the first line of the בָּרְכוּ while bowing as a sign of respect to God—the same way one might bow down toward a king or a queen. The congregation recites the second line of the prayer in response while bowing, too.

Practice reading the בָּרְכוּ aloud.

1. בָּרְכוּ אֶת־יְיָ הַמְבֹרָךְ.
2. בָּרוּךְ יְיָ הַמְבֹרָךְ לְעוֹלָם וָעֶד.

Praise Adonai, who is to be praised.
Praised is Adonai, who is to be praised forever and ever.

4

INTO THE TEXT

Ask students to read aloud the introduction to the prayer on page 4 of the text. You can vary the order in which students read the בָּרְכוּ by using the following techniques:

- Ask the entire class to read the בָּרְכוּ in unison.
- Ask individual students to read the בָּרְכוּ.
- Ask individual students to read the English meaning of the בָּרְכוּ.

Modeling Prayer

Direct the students to stand as a congregation. Select one student to be the leader and to chant the first Hebrew line of the prayer while bowing. (Make sure that this student is comfortable chanting and if not, select another student.) Then ask the congregation as a whole to respond by reciting the second line while bowing.

A CALL TO PRAYER

Tell the students: Now we are ready to think about the prayer that calls us to come together for the service as a community.

Display Word Card 1: בָּרְכוּ

The בָּרְכוּ marks the official start of the prayer service and is recited only when the community is present—when there is a מִנְיָן present. A מִנְיָן consists of at least ten community members age 12 or older for girls and 13 or older for boys; it represents the Jewish community in miniature. Our tradition emphasizes the importance of community, and therefore many prayers require the presence of the community before they can be recited.

Visualizing the Concept

Draw a second circle on the chalkboard. Draw ten lines radiating out from the circle. Select ten students and have each one come to the board and write his or her name on a line. Write the terms "community" and "מִנְיָן" in the center of the circle. Now add the name of the prayer, בָּרְכוּ, to the center of the circle.

Ask: What is the significance of praying as a community instead of as individuals? *(a shared Jewish prayer experience bonds individuals together; a shared experience provides the opportunity to take part in a universal Jewish tradition; a prayer community offers support for members who are ill, lonely, or grieving; a prayer community offers the opportunity for members to share joyous events in their lives)*

Add additional lines to the circle to include all class members and make the community complete.

PRAYER DICTIONARY

Word Cards

Display Word Cards 1–5 separately, in order. Ask students to read each one. Post the Word Cards in a pocket chart or on the edge of the chalkboard.

Call on students to read:

- each word ending with a letter that has a final form

  (בָּרוּךְ   הַמְבֹרָךְ   לְעוֹלָם)

- the word not pronounced as it looks (יְיָ)

- the word ending with a sounded vowel (בָּרְכוּ)

Display Word Cards 1, 3, and 4. These cards all contain related Hebrew words. Ask students to read each card and then to look up its meaning in the Prayer Dictionary on page 5. What is the common meaning of each word? ("praise")

Dictionary Review

Distribute Word Cards 1–5 randomly among the students. Have any student whose card has the word meaning "praise" hold up that card and read the word aloud. (בָּרְכוּ   הַמְבֹרָךְ   בָּרוּךְ).
Then ask any student whose card has a word meaning "God's name" (יְיָ) or "forever and ever" (לְעוֹלָם וָעֶד) to hold up that card and read the word aloud.

Ask students to complete page 5 independently. Review their answers.

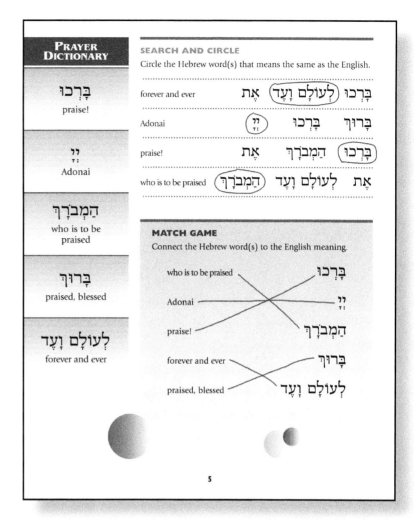

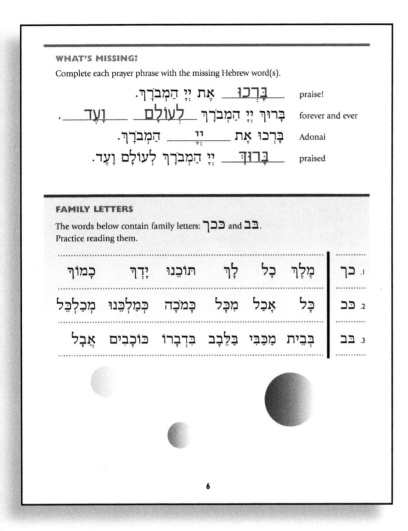

WHAT'S MISSING?

Complete each prayer phrase with the missing Hebrew word(s).

בָּרְכוּ _____ אֶת יְיָ הַמְבֹרָךְ.   praise!

בָּרוּךְ יְיָ הַמְבֹרָךְ _____ לְעוֹלָם _____ וָעֶד.   forever and ever

בָּרְכוּ אֶת _____ יְיָ _____ הַמְבֹרָךְ.   Adonai

בָּרוּךְ _____ יְיָ הַמְבֹרָךְ לְעוֹלָם וָעֶד.   praised

FAMILY LETTERS

The words below contain family letters: בּ בב and ךָ כ כּ.
Practice reading them.

כָּמוֹךָ	כָּל	כָּל	לָךְ	לְ	מֶלֶךְ	כָּל	תוֹכֵנוּ יָדְךָ	כך .1
מְכַלְכֵּל	כָּל	אֹכֶל	מִכָּל	כָּמָה	כְּמַלְכֵּנוּ	כָּל		כב .2
אָבֵל	כּוֹכָבִים	בִּדְבָרוֹ	בַּלֵּבָב	מַכַּבִּי	בֵּית			בב .3

6

Reading Skills

Direct students to underline words that contain two or more letters from the same family. *(line 1: 6th word; line 2: 4th, 5th, and 6th words; line 3: 1st, 3rd, 4th, and 5th words)* Ask students to circle, in every word, the letters that are members of both letter families. Have them include the vowel. Call on students to read each circled letter sound (with its vowel) and then to read the complete word.

WHAT'S MISSING?

Display Word Cards 1, 2, 4, and 5.

Direct students to complete page 6 of the textbook independently (they can use the Word Cards to help with meaning and spelling). Review the answers together. Then, for each answer, choose a student to identify and hold up the correct Word Card, so students can self-check their work.

Extending the Lesson

Display Word Cards 1–3 in mixed-up order. Call on students to place them in the correct right-to-left order to form the first line of the prayer. (Fill in the "missing" word אֶת on the board.) Repeat the exercise for the second line of the prayer with Word Cards 2–5. See "Reinforcing Word Order" on page 7 of this guide for variations of this activity.

FAMILY LETTERS
Alef Bet Review

Display an *alef bet* chart. Call on students to recite the *alef bet* in order. Then point to letters out of sequence and call on students to name these letters. Call out letter names and have students give their sounds. Call out letter names and ask students to point to them on the *alef bet* chart.

Dagesh (דָּגֵשׁ)—Dot in the Middle of a Letter

Explain that some groups of letters in the *alef bet* make up letter families. On the chalkboard write these sets of family letters: בּ בב כּ כך פּ פפ תּ ת. Talk about the similarity within each family (same shape) and the difference (the dot found in the middle of one member in each letter family). Discuss whether the dot—the *dagesh* in the middle of the letter—affects the sound of the letter in each pair.

Ask students for the names and sounds of the family letters found in the activity at the bottom of page 6.

IN THE SYNAGOGUE

Modeling Prayer

Read the page aloud together with the students. Then allow the students a few moments to practice reading the בָּרְכוּ with a partner.

Two By Two

Create larger "prayer groups" in the following way:

Step 1: Combine sets of partners (i.e., partners A & B with partners C & D; partners E & F with partners G & H; and so on). Select one student to be the leader of each newly combined group and the others to be members of the congregation. Ask each leader to chant the first line, and the congregants to answer.

Step 2: Combine groups once again, enlarging each prayer group from 4 to 8 members. Select a new leader and repeat the above process.

Step 3: Depending upon the size of your class, combine groups again (and perhaps again) until the entire class has been united in prayer.

For Discussion

Read the last sentence (in italics) on the page together. How do we indicate that we are ready to pray? *(our responses to the leader, our demeanor in synagogue, our active participation)*

IN THE SYNAGOGUE

How did the בָּרְכוּ get its name? בָּרְכוּ is the first word of the prayer. The first word of a Hebrew prayer is often the name by which the prayer is known.

The בָּרְכוּ is thousands of years old. The Jewish people have said the בָּרְכוּ since the time of the Temple—בֵּית הַמִּקְדָּשׁ. Today, in many congregations the leader of the service calls us to pray with the very same words that were recited in the Temple.

The cantor or rabbi chants

בָּרְכוּ אֶת־יְיָ הַמְבֹרָךְ.

and the congregation answers

בָּרוּךְ יְיָ הַמְבֹרָךְ לְעוֹלָם וָעֶד.

Just as we respond to a friendly "hello" with a greeting, we answer the בָּרְכוּ—the Call to Prayer—with the response that yes, we will pray.

7

Photo Op

Note: "Photo Op" offers teacher and students the opportunity to broaden class discussions by utilizing photographs that appear throughout the text.

The students in the photograph on page 7 have gathered for a student prayer service.

What is the name of the siddur used in your synagogue? Is there a special siddur your synagogue uses when there is a children's service? If so, what is the name of the children's siddur?

Extending the Opportunity

Bring siddurim into the classroom. Direct each student, or pairs of students, to take a siddur and help them locate the בָּרְכוּ. Chant the בָּרְכוּ together.

TRUE OR FALSE

Direct students to complete the exercise at the top of the page. Review answers by calling on students individually, asking them if the answer is true or false. Then direct them to change one word in each false sentence to make the sentence true. *(sentence 2: first—not last—word; sentence 4: old or ancient—not new—prayer)*

DISCOVER THE PRAYER

Direct students to complete the activity.

ROOTS

Explain that family letters are really the *same* letter in different forms, but that different members of the same family can have different sounds. Write the three letters בּ ר כ on the chalkboard in the manner shown below. Call on individual students to write on the board the family letters for בּ and for כ under each letter:

write on board ⟶ כ   ר   בּ

students write ⟶ כּ   ב

ך

Complete the "Roots" exercise together.

Visualizing the Concept

Help your students understand Hebrew roots:

- Draw a simple tree with three roots and three (or more) branches.

- Using colored chalk, write the Hebrew letters בּ ר כ on the roots—one letter on each root.

- On the branches write the three words in this lesson that are built on this root (one word on each branch): בָּרְכוּ, הַמְבֹרָךְ, בָּרוּךְ. Make the three root letters in each word the same color as the root letters at the bottom of the tree. Write the remaining letters of the words, and the vowels, in white.

- Discuss the English meaning of the words with the class. *(all have to do with praising or blessing God)*

The Fruit of the Tree

Create a tree with three roots from oaktag or poster board. On each of the three roots write one root letter (בּ ר כ). Then write the meaning of the root ("bless," "praise") on the trunk of the tree. If possible, laminate the tree.

Next, put fruit on the tree. Begin by creating three fruit-shaped pieces of paper, one for each of the three words in the lesson that are built on the root. Choose any type of fruit—make three oranges for an orange tree out of orange paper, or three bananas for a banana tree out of yellow paper, or three apples for an apple tree out of red paper. On each piece of fruit write a different Hebrew word based on that root. If possible, laminate each piece of fruit. Use velcro or Fun-Tac to attach the fruit to the tree.

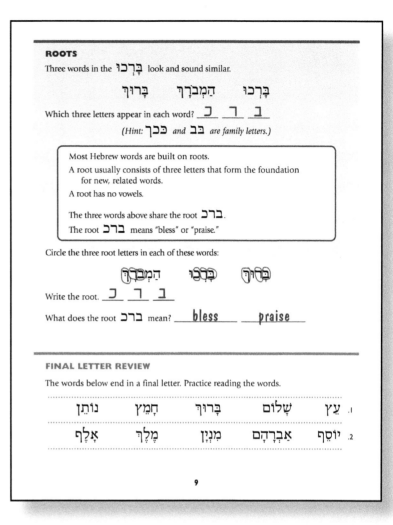

- Each time students learn a new word built on this root, make a new piece of the same type of fruit, write the word on it, and add it to the tree.

- Each time you introduce a new root, create a new tree using the new root letters at the root of the tree and writing the meaning of the root on the trunk of the tree.

Note: The fruit is removable so it can be used for games and review activities later.

Practice reading the Torah blessing.

1. בָּרְכוּ אֶת־יְיָ הַמְבֹרָךְ.

2. בָּרוּךְ יְיָ הַמְבֹרָךְ לְעוֹלָם וָעֶד.

3. בָּרוּךְ אַתָּה, יְיָ אֱלֹהֵינוּ, מֶלֶךְ הָעוֹלָם,

4. אֲשֶׁר בָּחַר בָּנוּ מִכָּל הָעַמִּים, וְנָתַן לָנוּ אֶת תּוֹרָתוֹ.

5. בָּרוּךְ אַתָּה, יְיָ, נוֹתֵן הַתּוֹרָה.

Why do you think the בָּרְכוּ was made a part of the Torah blessing?

_____

_____

_____

10

TORAH BLESSING

Call on students to read lines 1 and 2.

Reinforce reading skills before calling on students to read all five lines. Ask students for:

- the correct pronunciation of מִכָּל (the 4th word on line 4—"oh" or "aw" vowel sound)

- the words in lines 1, 2, 3, and 5 that are built on the root that means "praise"(ב ר כ)

- words with a *dagesh*

- words with final letters

Modeling Prayer

To practice the blessing, lead the class in reading the complete blessing in unison. Then call on individual students to read it. You may wish to teach students to chant it as well.

As an alternative reading exercise, appoint a student leader. Ask the leader to recite line 1, and have the rest of the class respond as the congregation and recite line 2. The leader should then repeat line 2 and continue with lines 3–5.

Note: When the בָּרְכוּ is part of the Torah blessing, the melody is different.

Discuss the answers to the question at the bottom of page 10.

Helpful Hint: Think about the purpose of the בָּרְכוּ in the prayer service, and review the introductory material on page 4 of the textbook. (*the* בָּרְכוּ *calls the congregation together for prayer and announces that the main part of the service is about to begin; the* בָּרְכוּ *introduces the Torah blessing for the same reason: to call the congregation together for the Torah reading and to announce when each aliyah is about to begin*)

The Fruit of the Tree

Introduce the students to the Hebrew word for "blessing"— בְּרָכָה. Write the word on the chalkboard. Challenge students to recognize the root letters and give the meaning of the root ("bless," "praise"). If you have used the fruit tree from page 19 of this guide, add another fruit to the כ ר ב tree: בְּרָכָה.

GOD'S NAME

Discuss the correct pronunciation of God's name: Adonai ("eye" ending). Use this opportunity to reinforce the "eye" ending in other words: אַ and אָ are sometimes followed by *yud* (י) at the end of a word (אַי and אָי). אַי and אָי have the sound "eye."

Extending the Lesson

Distribute siddurim to the students. Have students work in partnerships to find and read God's name. (*Adonai*)

READING PRACTICE

Write the following on the chalkboard: ב כ פ. Then write these letters again, adding the *dagesh* to change the sound: בּ כּ פּ. Explain that the *dagesh* changes the sound in certain letters; in many others a *dagesh* in a letter does not change the sound. Write the following examples on the board without a *dagesh*, and have the students read the sound each letter makes:

ז מ י ל ס ג

Now add the *dagesh* and call on students to read the sounds once again:

זּ מּ יּ לּ סּ גּ

Direct students to lines 1–6 at the bottom of page 11.

- Ask them to circle or highlight each letter in lines 3, 4, and 6 that has a *dagesh* that does *not* change the sound of the letter (e.g., line 3 —גָּדוֹל).

- Ask them to circle God's name in each line and pronounce it correctly.

READING PRACTICE

Practice reading the following sentences. Circle God's name wherever it appears.

١. בָּרְכוּ אֶת יְיָ הַמְבֹרָךְ.

٢. בָּרוּךְ יְיָ הַמְבֹרָךְ לְעוֹלָם וָעֶד.

٣. מֵאֵין כָּמוֹךָ, יְהֹוָה גָּדוֹל אַתָּה וְגָדוֹל שִׁמְךָ בִּגְבוּרָה.

٤. כִּי לְךָ הַגְּדֻלָּה וְהַגְּבוּרָה וְהַתִּפְאֶרֶת.

٥. יְיָ צְבָאוֹת שְׁמוֹ.

٦. גָּדוֹל ה' וּמְהֻלָּל מְאֹד, וְלִגְדֻלָּתוֹ אֵין חֵקֶר.

11

Teamwork

Divide the class into two teams. Assign lines 1, 3, and 5 to one team and lines 2, 4, and 6 to the other. Have each team meet and practice its assigned lines. Teammates should help one another with pronunciation. Ask each team to read its assigned lines aloud to the rest of the class, in unison. Then, ask individual team members to read the lines. After the first team is done, ask the other team to repeat the activity for its lines.

HOW WOULD YOU RESPOND?

Allow students adequate time to write their responses to the items on page 12. Then ask them to share their responses with the class.

Photo Op

Direct students to the listing of sounds under the heading "You Hear" found above the photo. Ask students:

- Which sound is depicted in the photo? (*latkes sizzling in oil*)

- Which holiday comes to mind? (*Ḥanukkah*)

The page 12 worksheet reproduced:

HOW WOULD YOU RESPOND?

In the בָּרְכוּ the leader of the service *calls* us to pray. We *hear* and we *answer*: "Yes, we will pray."

In each example below, tell how you would respond.

YOU HEAR:	YOU DO OR SAY:
The doorbell ringing	_____
"Shabbat shalom"	_____
Mom calling	_____
A neighbor struggling with heavy packages	_____
Latkes sizzling in oil	_____
The blast of the shofar	_____
The alarm clock buzzing	_____
Haman's name	_____

בָּרְכוּ אֶת־יְיָ הַמְבֹרָךְ   בָּרוּךְ יְיָ הַמְבֹרָךְ לְעוֹלָם וָעֶד

12

FLUENT READING

Conduct a "Word Search." Ask your students to become detectives and to search for words that reflect specific reading skills they have acquired. Each time they find a word that reflects the skill, they should read the word aloud and also read the complete phrase or line containing the word. Conduct separate Word Searches for:

- words with a *dagesh*
- words with final letters
- God's name, *Adonai*
- words in which the letter *yud* is pronounced (examples: line 4—יִתֵּן, line 5—יִשְׂרָאֵל)
- words built on the root ב ר כ

The Fruit of the Tree

Challenge students to find the words built on the root ב ר כ that are new on this page.

Add the words to the fruit of your ב ר כ tree.

Tic-Tac-Toe

Draw a Tic-Tac-Toe grid on the chalkboard. Write the numbers 1 through 9 randomly, one in each box of the Tic-Tac-Toe board. Divide the class into two teams: א and ב.

Have each team alternate, with a member of each team selecting a box and reading the corresponding line on page 13 of the textbook. If the line is read correctly, the player places his or her team mark (א or ב) in the box. Decide on specific rules ahead of time: whether mistakes are allowed, whether self-correction is allowed, etc. The first team to score Tic-Tac-Toe wins.

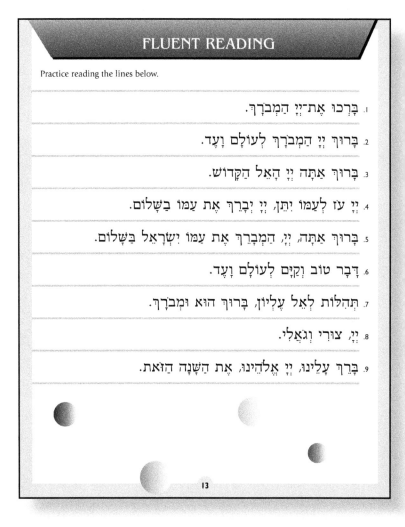

FLUENT READING

Practice reading the lines below.

1. בָּרְכוּ אֶת־יְיָ הַמְבֹרָךְ.

2. בָּרוּךְ יְיָ הַמְבֹרָךְ לְעוֹלָם וָעֶד.

3. בָּרוּךְ אַתָּה יְיָ הָאֵל הַקָּדוֹשׁ.

4. יְיָ עֹז לְעַמּוֹ יִתֵּן, יְיָ יְבָרֵךְ אֶת עַמּוֹ בַשָּׁלוֹם.

5. בָּרוּךְ אַתָּה, יְיָ, הַמְבָרֵךְ אֶת עַמּוֹ יִשְׂרָאֵל בַּשָּׁלוֹם.

6. דָּבָר טוֹב וְקַיָּם לְעוֹלָם וָעֶד.

7. תְּהִלּוֹת לְאֵל עֶלְיוֹן, בָּרוּךְ הוּא וּמְבֹרָךְ.

8. יְיָ, צוּרִי וְגֹאֲלִי.

9. בָּרֵךְ עָלֵינוּ, יְיָ אֱלֹהֵינוּ, אֶת הַשָּׁנָה הַזֹּאת.

13

WORKSHEET

Hand each student a copy of the worksheet for Lesson 1 to review the בָּרְכוּ.

FAMILY EDUCATION

Duplicate and send home with students the Family Education page, "As a Family: Coming Together in Community" (at the back of this guide), to reach out to the students' families and broaden the sense of community. You may also choose to invite parents to "drop in" for the first or last few minutes of class to review the prayer with their children. Consider extending this invitation periodically throughout the year.

Name: _____

בָּרְכוּ

1. Complete the בָּרְכוּ by adding the missing words. Select your words from the box.

הַמְבֹרָךְ	בָּרְכוּ	בָּרוּךְ	

_____ אֶת יְיָ _____.

_____ יְיָ _____ לְעוֹלָם וָעֶד.

2. Write the root letters of the three missing words in the above exercise. ____ ____ ____

3. What is the meaning of this root? _____ _____

4. How many people are needed to form a מִנְיָן? _____

   How old must one be to be counted as part of a מִנְיָן?

   _____

5. How do you pronounce God's name: יְהֹוָד, יְיָ? _____

6. Explain in your own words the purpose of the בָּרְכוּ.

   _____

   _____

7. Why do we need a מִנְיָן to recite the בָּרְכוּ?

(Hint: Think about the significance of a מִנְיָן. Think about the purpose of the בָּרְכוּ.)

   _____

   _____

LESSON 2

מַעֲרִיב עֲרָבִים / יוֹצֵר אוֹר

LEARNING OBJECTIVES

Prayer Reading Skills

Distinguishing between צ and ע

Root: ע ר ב ("evening")

A double-duty dot

Prayer Concepts

First blessing before the Shema:

- "partner prayers": אוֹר מַעֲרִיב עֲרָבִים and יוֹצֵר

- the evening and morning prayers praise God, who creates night and day

- creation is renewed each day

- God is the Creator of peace and of all things

Second blessing before the Shema:

- "partner prayers": בָה רַבָּה אַהֲבַת עוֹלָם and אַהֲ

- the evening and morning prayers reflect God's love for humanity

- God shows God's love for us by giving us the Torah and mitzvot

ABOUT THE PRAYER

We recite two blessings before the Shema. The first blessing of the evening service praises God for creating the twilight followed by darkness. The first blessing of the morning service praises God for creating the morning light and renewed energy. The rhythm of these prayers reflects the story of creation in Genesis 1:1—"there was darkness over the surface . . . and God said, 'Let there be light' . . . God separated the light from the darkness. God called the light Day and the darkness God called Night. And there was evening and there was morning, a first day."

The second blessing of the evening and morning services praises God for God's unending love for the Jewish people.

INSTRUCTIONAL MATERIALS

Textbook pages 14–23

Word Cards 6–16

Worksheet for Lesson 2

Family Education: "As a Family: Evening and Morning" (at the back of this guide)

SET INDUCTION

Divide students into two groups: "Night" and "Day." Give each group a large circle cut from construction paper or oaktag: Night should get black or a dark color; Day should get white or a light color. Explain that the circle symbolizes the continuous cycle of time. Then give each group 7–10 pieces of white index-card-size paper.

Write the following statements on the chalkboard:

- Because there is Night . . .

- Because there is Day . . .

Ask each group to develop at least five responses to each statement, and to write their responses on the white index-card-size pieces of paper and paste or tape them onto their circle. (*possible responses: Night—rest, renewal of strength, time for reflection, cooling the earth, nocturnal animals, viewing heavenly bodies . . . Day—growth, play, warming the earth, working . . .*)

Ask: Which do you prefer, Night or Day? (*individual answers*) Ask why.

מַעֲרִיב עֲרָבִים/ יוֹצֵר אוֹר

מַעֲרִיב עֲרָבִים

What's your favorite part of the day—morning or evening? Maybe you love the evening! The sun turns from yellow to red, the clouds turn pink, and a beautiful, deep blue-purple spreads across the sky. You can see the first stars start to twinkle as night moves in, and there's a feeling of calm and peace, as if the whole world were settling down to rest. The מַעֲרִיב עֲרָבִים prayer is said every day as daylight turns to evening. It praises God for creating the twilight and the darkness—every single day.

Practice reading these lines from מַעֲרִיב עֲרָבִים.

1. בָּרוּךְ אַתָּה, יְיָ אֱלֹהֵינוּ, מֶלֶךְ הָעוֹלָם,
   אֲשֶׁר בִּדְבָרוֹ מַעֲרִיב עֲרָבִים.

2. אֵל חַי וְקַיָּם, תָּמִיד יִמְלֹךְ עָלֵינוּ, לְעוֹלָם וָעֶד.
   בָּרוּךְ אַתָּה, יְיָ, הַמַּעֲרִיב עֲרָבִים.

Praised are You, Adonai our God, Ruler of the world, whose word brings on the evening.

May the living and eternal God rule over us always. Praised are You, Adonai, who brings on the evening.

14

INTO THE TEXT

Call on students to read the introduction to the prayer on page 14.

Think About It!

What is good about having a period of twilight before the darkness of evening? (*allows us to slowly adjust to the darkness; prepares the earth and its inhabitants to slow down for rest, like cooling down after strenuous exercise; displays the beautiful colors of the evening sky*)

Direct students to the two sentences of the prayer. The first sentence introduces the prayer. The second sentence concludes the prayer.

Divide the class into two groups—א and ב. Ask group א to read the first Hebrew sentence. Ask group ב to read the English meaning of the sentence. Then ask group ב to read the second Hebrew sentence and group א to read its English meaning. Then have the groups switch sentences.

Call on individual students to read each Hebrew sentence.

Artistic Expression

Provide crayons, markers, or paints and ask students to draw or paint an image of the colors of the evening sky. Give them five to ten minutes to do so. Display their work on the classroom wall, and label the collection מַעֲרִיב עֲרָבִים.

PRAYER DICTIONARY

Word Cards

Display Word Cards 6–9 in random order. Ask students to read each one. Which Word Card contains the name of the evening blessing? (מַעֲרִיב עֲרָבִים) Turn the Word Cards over and read the meaning of the phrase. *(brings on the evening)* Direct students to lightly circle the Hebrew phrase and its English meaning on the bottom half of page 14 in the textbook.

Which Word Card means "living" or "lives"? (חַי) Student hint: The word is related to the term we use at special celebrations when we traditionally clink glasses and say לְחַיִּים— "to life."

Which Word Card means "will rule"? (יִמְלֹךְ)

Direct students to complete the "Word Match" and "Complete the Phrase" exercises. Review answers or walk around the room to assess student work.

SING ALONG!

Read the words of the song aloud with the class. If you are comfortable, sing it together with the class, or bring in a tape of the song and ask students to sing along with it.

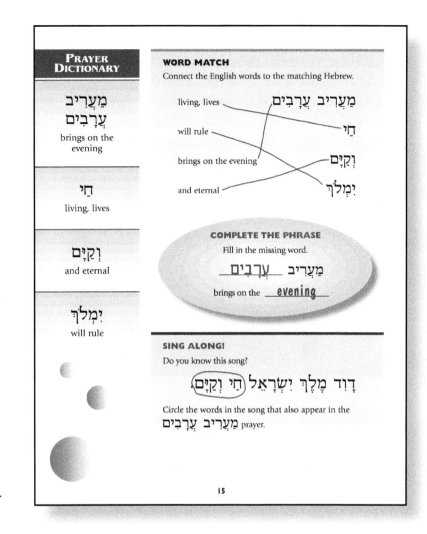

IN THE SYNAGOGUE

מַעֲרִיב עֲרָבִים is said before the *evening* Shema prayer; it has a "partner prayer" that is said before the *morning* Shema. You will learn about the partner prayer—יוֹצֵר אוֹר—in the second part of this chapter, and you will learn about the Shema itself in the next chapter.

מַעֲרִיב עֲרָבִים and יוֹצֵר אוֹר are linked because they remind us that God creates both morning and night, light and darkness. And we praise God for bringing us morning after night after morning . . . day after day after day.

Why do you think we need to say a prayer praising God's creations both in the evening and *in the morning?*

READING PRACTICE

Practice reading the words below. Watch for the differences between ע and צ!

1. צִיצִית מַעֲרִיב מַצָּה עִבְרִית מִצְוָה עֶרֶב
2. עֲרָבִים עֲבוֹדָה הַמּוֹצִיא צְדָקָה הָעֵץ צַדִּיק

16

READING PRACTICE

Divide the class into two teams by counting off צ ע צ ע צ ע... (instead of 1–2, 1–2, 1–2 . . .)

Ask all those in the ע team to circle or highlight in their textbooks all the words containing the letter ע. Ask all those in the צ team to circle or highlight in their textbooks all the words containing the letter צ.

Ask: Which word has an *ayin* and a *tsadee*? (הָעֵץ)

Ask each group to read the words they have circled. First ask the group to read them in unison, then call on students individually to read the words. You can ask one student to read all the words, or go around the class asking each student in a team to read one word, with the next student reading the next word.

Change the assignment: Repeat this procedure, but with each group, or individual students, reading the words they have *not* circled or highlighted.

IN THE SYNAGOGUE

Count off 1–2, 1–2, 1–2 . . . around the classroom; make each 1–2 group a partnership of two students. Ask each set of partners to read "In the Synagogue" together and to pose one question based on the paragraph. (*e.g., when is* מַעֲרִיב עֲרָבִים *recited?*) Call on each partnership to read its question to the entire class, and ask the class to respond to the question to reinforce the material.

Discuss the question found in italics at the conclusion of "In the Synagogue." *(God creates each part of the day—both the darkness and the light and all that lives; reciting a prayer both in the evening and the morning indicates our appreciation of all of creation)*

Photo Op

Ask students:

- What time of the day is depicted? (*twilight; sunset*)
- What are the people doing? (*rowing; fishing*)
- Why do you think they might enjoy this time of day? (*calm, peaceful; opportunity to appreciate the setting sun and cycle of time*)
- Think of the most beautiful sunset you've seen. Which colors filled the sky? How did you feel at the time? How do you feel as you think about it?

ROOTS

Read and complete the section with students.

The Fruit of the Tree

Create a new oaktag fruit tree with three roots. Write the root letters ע ר ב on the three roots—one letter on each root. Write the meaning ("evening") on the trunk of the tree. Create pieces of fruit for the tree (a fruit you haven't used yet)—one for each word built on the root found on page 17. (מַעֲרִיב עֲרָבִים)

Student Challenge:

• Ask students: Which word do we use to indicate the evening when Shabbat or a holiday begins? (עֶרֶב)

• Add the word to the tree.

• Ask students for phrases with עֶרֶב and add the phrases to the tree.

(עֶרֶב שַׁבָּת   עֶרֶב רֹאשׁ הַשָּׁנָה   עֶרֶב פֶּסַח)

THINK ABOUT THIS!

Allow your class a few moments to consider possible responses before calling upon them to share their ideas with classmates. (*reinforces the notion that it is God who creates the cycle of time; announces the theme of the prayer, and restates that theme at the end; reminds us of the power and importance of God*)

ROOTS

Two words in מַעֲרִיב עֲרָבִים look and sound similar.

מַעֲרִיב   עֲרָבִים

> Most Hebrew words are built on roots.
> A root usually consists of three letters.
>
> The two words above share the root ערב.
> ערב means "evening."
>
> Write the root. ב   ר   ע
>
> What does the root ערב mean? __evening__

Circle the two words with the root ערב—"evening"—in each sentence below.

1. בָּרוּךְ אַתָּה, יְיָ אֱלֹהֵינוּ, מֶלֶךְ הָעוֹלָם, אֲשֶׁר בִּדְבָרוֹ (מַעֲרִיב) (עֲרָבִים) . . .

2. בָּרוּךְ אַתָּה, יְיָ, (הַמַּעֲרִיב) (עֲרָבִים).

Think About This!

Why do you think the prayer begins *and* ends with the statement that God brings on the evening—מַעֲרִיב עֲרָבִים?

17

יוֹצֵר אוֹר

Maybe you love the daytime. One of the best things about the morning is that it means a new chance to have fun, to learn, and to do something special. Maybe there's a new kid at school you've been waiting to meet, or a soccer match after school. The יוֹצֵר אוֹר prayer is said every morning to praise God for creating the morning light, for giving us renewed energy, and for bringing us the blessing of another day to do good things.

Practice reading these lines from יוֹצֵר אוֹר.

1. בָּרוּךְ אַתָּה, יְיָ אֱלֹהֵינוּ, מֶלֶךְ הָעוֹלָם, יוֹצֵר אוֹר וּבוֹרֵא חֹשֶׁךְ, עֹשֶׂה שָׁלוֹם וּבוֹרֵא אֶת הַכֹּל.

2. בָּרוּךְ אַתָּה, יְיָ, יוֹצֵר הַמְּאוֹרוֹת.

Praised are You, Adonai our God, Ruler of the world, who forms light and creates darkness, who makes peace and creates all things.

Praised are You, Adonai, who forms the lights.

18

INTO THE TEXT

Explain to students that יוֹצֵר אוֹר is the "partner prayer" to מַעֲרִיב עֲרָבִים. יוֹצֵר אוֹר is the first blessing before the morning Shema. Call on students to read the introduction to the prayer on page 18 of their textbooks.

Personalizing the Prayer

Ask students to describe a very special day in their own lives. Then have them recite the יוֹצֵר אוֹר prayer.

Direct students' attention to the two sentences of the prayer on page 18 of the textbook. The first line introduces the prayer; the second line concludes it.

Divide the class into two groups, א and ב. Ask group א to read sentence 1 aloud in Hebrew. Then ask group ב to read aloud its English meaning at the bottom of the page. Ask group ב to read sentence 2 aloud in Hebrew. Then ask group א to read aloud its English meaning at the bottom of the page. Then have the groups switch sentences.

Call on individual students to read each Hebrew sentence.

Artistic Expression

Using crayons, markers, or paints, ask students to draw an image of light breaking through the darkness at dawn. Collect the artwork and post it on the classroom wall. Label the display יוֹצֵר אוֹר.

PRAYER DICTIONARY

Word Cards

Display Word Cards 10–16 in random order. Call on students to read each one in turn, and provide them with the English meaning from the back of the Word Card. Then, challenge students to read each card in random order and to give the English meaning without looking at the back of the Word Card.

Call on students to form the following phrases with the Word Cards: "forms light" (יוֹצֵר אוֹר), "and creates darkness" (וּבוֹרֵא חֹשֶׁךְ), "makes peace" (עֹשֶׂה שָׁלוֹם).

Direct students to the second sentence of the prayer on page 18. Ask them to circle the word that means "forms." (יוֹצֵר)

Ask students to complete the "Phrase Match" and "What's Missing?" exercises on page 19 of the textbook. Walk around the room to assess students' work.

Night and Day

Divide the class into two sections: "Night" and "Day." Call on Night students to read sentences 1 and 2 on page 14, each sentence in Hebrew followed immediately by its English meaning. Then ask Day students to read sentences 1 and 2 on page 18, each sentence in Hebrew followed immediately by its English meaning.

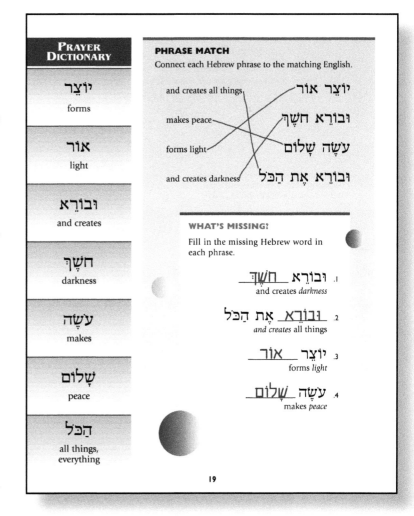

CREATION CONTINUES

Both יוֹצֵר אוֹר and מַעֲרִיב עֲרָבִים praise God, the Creator, and describe some of the things that God creates.

This is what יוֹצֵר אוֹר and מַעֲרִיב עֲרָבִים say God does:

1. מַעֲרִיב עֲרָבִים
brings on the evening

2. יוֹצֵר אוֹר
forms light

3. בּוֹרֵא חֹשֶׁךְ
creates darkness

4. עֹשֶׂה שָׁלוֹם
makes peace

5. בּוֹרֵא אֶת הַכֹּל
creates all things

Why do you think the prayers include so many words that mean "create"? What does that tell us about God?

_____

_____

_____

A DOUBLE-DUTY DOT

Sometimes the dot for שׁ (shin) and שׂ (sin) identifies the letter *and* the vowel "וֹ".

Read each word below.

קָדֹשׁ וַיַּחֲשֹׁף מֹשֶׁה שָׁלֹשׁ חֹשֶׁךְ

20

A DOUBLE-DUTY DOT

Write the word חֹשֶׁךְ on the chalkboard. Draw a circle around the dot in the word-part חֹשׁ. Explain that this dot is a double-duty dot because it has two jobs. The dot indicates that the letter שׁ is a *shin*; the dot is also the vowel for the letter ח.

Write the following on the chalkboard:

קָדְשִׁים שְׁלֹשֶׁת לִפְרֹשׁ מֹשֶׁה

Call on students to circle the double-duty dot in each word. Then call on students to read each word.

Repeat the above technique for *sin*, using the word שֹׂרֶק.

Write the following on the chalkboard:

וְשָׂשֹׂן חָשַׂף

Call on students to circle the double-duty dot in the words. Then call on students to read the words.

Direct students to the bottom of page 20. Ask them to circle the double-duty dot in each word. Then ask them: Which is the only word with a double-duty dot for the letter *sin*? (וַיַּחֲשֹׂף) Ask them to read each word aloud.

Which word with a double-duty dot is found in a phrase in the prayer יוֹצֵר אוֹר? (חֹשֶׁךְ) What is its English meaning? *(darkness)*

CREATION CONTINUES

Read the introduction with students. Call on individual students and ask them to read aloud each phrase and its English meaning. Which word means "creates"? (בּוֹרֵא)

Read the two phrases with בּוֹרֵא. Ask the students: Which words in the other three phrases have meanings similar to "creates"? (מַעֲרִיב יוֹצֵר עֹשֶׂה)

Read aloud the two questions in the yellow circle next to the Hebrew phrases. Divide the class into groups of two or three, and allow the groups a few moments to discuss the questions with a partner and write their responses on the lines. Call on partners to share their answers. *(Question 1: the variety of the words for "create" symbolizes the variety of things that God created; creating different kinds of things requires different kinds of creation by God; God creates through varying means. Question 2: God is filled with a wider range of creative force than we can imagine; no single word is adequate to describe the creative powers of God)*

Extending the Discussion

The prayer says God "makes peace"— עֹשֶׂה שָׁלוֹם. Remind the students that we are all made in the image of God and we can do God-like actions. Ask them: What can we do to help make peace? *(extend a hand in friendship; talk out problems rather than fight over them; share decision making; find ways to resolve conflicts before they become fights)*

IN THE SYNAGOGUE

Ask individual students to read the following passages:

- the introduction

- the section describing the first blessing before the Shema

- the section describing the second blessing before the Shema

A Midrash

God, wanting to give the Torah to the Israelites, asked what guarantee the people would give that the Torah would be cared for. First the Israelites offered their ancestors, then the prophets, but only when they promised that the Torah would be passed down and taught to each generation of children throughout the ages did God know that the people understood the importance of the gift. So God offered them the Torah and they accepted.

THINK ABOUT THIS!

Discuss the question with the students. Encourage students to share their insights with classmates. (*declaring our love in return shows God that we understand the significance of this gift and the significance of God's love in choosing us to receive Torah; declaring our love for God is a way of saying "yes," we accept the responsibility of Torah*)

IN THE SYNAGOGUE

There are *two* blessings before the Shema prayer, which you will learn about in the next chapter. Each blessing has an *evening* and a *morning* version. You have already learned the first blessing before the Shema.

First blessing before the Shema
This blessing celebrates the wonder of creation and its renewal each day.

Evening blessing: מַעֲרִיב עֲרָבִים

Morning blessing: יוֹצֵר אוֹר

We also say a second blessing before the Shema.

Second blessing before the Shema
This blessing thanks God for giving us the Torah and mitzvot and—in this way—for showing us love.

Evening blessing: אַהֲבַת עוֹלָם

Morning blessing: אַהֲבָה רַבָּה

After the Shema comes the Ve'ahavta prayer—when we declare *our* love for *God*!

Think About This!
Why do you think we need to declare *our* love for God after describing God's love for *us*?

DRAW THE TIME
Draw a moon and stars above the name of the creation blessing we say at night.

Draw a sun above the name of the creation blessing we say in the morning.

מַעֲרִיב עֲרָבִים   יוֹצֵר אוֹר

21

A COMMON WORD

אוֹר   means "light."

הַמְּאוֹרוֹת   means "the lights."

Circle אוֹר within the word הַמְּ(אוֹר)וֹת.

What are "the lights" that God creates each day?

_____

THINK ABOUT THIS!

Which word or phrase do you consider to be the most important
in מַעֲרִיב עֲרָבִים? Write it here. _____

Which word or phrase do you consider to be the most important
in יוֹצֵר אוֹר? Write it here. _____

Why did you choose these words or phrases?

22

A COMMON WORD

Direct students to read and complete the activity.
(sun, moon, stars, lights from planets and other heavenly bodies)

THINK ABOUT THIS!

Allow students time to consider their individual responses and write them on the page. Call on each student to share his or her point of view, and invite class discussion. Make sure to ask "why."

FLUENT READING

Write the numbers 1–10 on ten slips of paper, fold them, and place them in a box. Each number will represent a line in "Fluent Reading." Ask ten students to each select a slip of paper. (If there are more than ten students in your class, create two number 1s, two number 2s, etc.) All those with odd numbers (1, 3, 5, 7, 9) will form one group, and all those with even numbers (2, 4, 6, 8, 10) will form another. You may choose to create three groups and divide up the lines accordingly.

The even group will be responsible for reading the even-numbered lines, and the odd group, the odd-numbered lines. Have each group practice its assigned lines; group members should assist each other. Ask each group to read its lines aloud, first in unison, and then with individual group members reading each line.

WORKSHEET

Duplicate the worksheet for Lesson 2. Use it to review the themes of the prayers in this lesson.

FAMILY EDUCATION

Duplicate and send home with students the Family Education page, "As a Family: Evening and Morning" (at the back of this guide), to heighten awareness of our appreciation of the cycle of time.

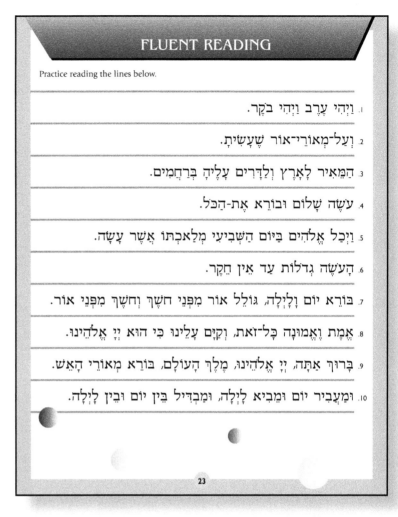

FLUENT READING

Practice reading the lines below.

1. וַיְהִי עֶרֶב וַיְהִי בֹקֶר.

2. וְעַל־מְאוֹרֵי־אוֹר שֶׁעָשִׂיתָ.

3. הַמֵּאִיר לָאָרֶץ וְלַדָּרִים עָלֶיהָ בְּרַחֲמִים.

4. עֹשֶׂה שָׁלוֹם וּבוֹרֵא אֶת־הַכֹּל.

5. וַיְכַל אֱלֹהִים בַּיוֹם הַשְּׁבִיעִי מְלַאכְתּוֹ אֲשֶׁר עָשָׂה.

6. הָעֹשֶׂה גְדֹלוֹת עַד אֵין חֵקֶר.

7. בּוֹרֵא יוֹם וָלָיְלָה, גּוֹלֵל אוֹר מִפְּנֵי חֹשֶׁךְ וְחֹשֶׁךְ מִפְּנֵי אוֹר.

8. אֱמֶת וֶאֱמוּנָה כָּל־זֹאת, וְקַיָּם עָלֵינוּ כִּי הוּא יְיָ אֱלֹהֵינוּ.

9. בָּרוּךְ אַתָּה, יְיָ אֱלֹהֵינוּ, מֶלֶךְ הָעוֹלָם, בּוֹרֵא מְאוֹרֵי הָאֵשׁ.

10. וּמַעֲבִיר יוֹם וּמֵבִיא לָיְלָה, וּמַבְדִּיל בֵּין יוֹם וּבֵין לָיְלָה.

23

Name: _____

מַעֲרִיב עֲרָבִים / יוֹצֵר אוֹר

1. At what time of day do we recite מַעֲרִיב עֲרָבִים? _____

2. For what do we praise God in מַעֲרִיב עֲרָבִים? _____

3. At what time of day do we recite יוֹצֵר אוֹר? _____

4. For what do we praise God in יוֹצֵר אוֹר? _____

5. What does the root ערב mean? _____

6. What does the word אוֹר mean? _____

7. The blessings אַהֲבָה רַבָּה and אַהֲבַת עוֹלָם speak of God's love for us.

   How is Torah a symbol of God's love?

   _____

   _____

8. Write the correct number next to the matching English phrase.

   _____ forms light   1. עֹשֶׂה שָׁלוֹם

   _____ makes peace   2. מַעֲרִיב עֲרָבִים

   _____ and creates all things   3. וּבוֹרֵא חֹשֶׁךְ

   _____ brings on the evening   4. יוֹצֵר אוֹר

   _____ and creates darkness   5. וּבוֹרֵא אֶת הַכֹּל

LESSON שְׁמַע 3

LEARNING OBJECTIVES

Prayer Reading Skills

Family letters: שׂ שׁ

Word Endings: נוּ ("us," "our"), וֹ ("his")

Root: כ ל מ ("rule")

Prayer Concepts

Pledge of loyalty

Core of our faith

Belief in one God

We can each be a witness (עֵד) to the oneness of God

Meaning of the term יִשְׂרָאֵל ("a people," "a state")

The response (second line) to the Shema: Blessed is the name of God's glorious kingdom forever and ever

Ethical Echoes:

- All Israel is responsible for one another
- A good name

BEYOND THE TEXTBOOK

Double-duty dot

Double dots

Double letters with *sh'va*

ABOUT THE PRAYER

The שְׁמַע comes directly from the Torah (Deuteronomy 6:4). The שְׁמַע is a statement of faith and allegiance to God. When we recite the words of the שְׁמַע, we affirm our belief in one God—Adonai.

The second sentence of the שְׁמַע was first said in the ancient Temple in Jerusalem; it was the response given by the people after hearing the Divine Name pronounced by the High Priests. Later it became the response to the first line of the שְׁמַע. Traditionally, this line has been recited silently or in a soft voice, to distinguish it from the biblical passages of the שְׁמַע. Its purpose is to affirm that, although Jews have lived under many kings and queens, God is the only Supreme Ruler of Israel. When Jews say this line, they publicly declare the uniqueness of God.

INSTRUCTIONAL MATERIALS

Text pages 24–33

Word Cards 2, 4, 5, 17–23

Worksheet for Lesson 3

Family Education: "Preparation for Name Day" and "As a Family: Name Day" (at the back of this guide)

SET INDUCTION

The Pledge

Ask students if they know the Pledge of Allegiance. Ask:

- What does the term "Pledge of Allegiance" mean? (*promise of loyalty; commitment*)
- Why do we recite the Pledge of Allegiance? (*connection to our country; love of our country; loyalty to our country*)
- What rituals do we follow when we recite the Pledge of Allegiance? (*stand; right hand on heart*)

Discuss with your class:

- occasions when other types of pledges are recited. (*Girl Scout and Boy Scout meetings; testimony in a court of law; taking oath of office for public office; becoming a citizen*)
- the significance of reciting a pledge in each of these instances. (*a promise of loyalty; a commitment of support; adherence to specific rules and regulations*)

If possible, invite to class people who have participated in such events to talk about what their pledges meant to them.

Explain that the שְׁמַע is our pledge of loyalty—of allegiance—to God. It is our statement of acceptance of one God, Adonai. It is our promise of allegiance to Judaism and to the Jewish people.

For Discussion

What actions can you take to demonstrate the sincerity of your pledge? (*be respectful of God's name; recite the שְׁמַע in a respectful manner; conduct oneself with the understanding that each person is made in the image of God; do not worship other gods or allow other temptations to become overwhelming*)

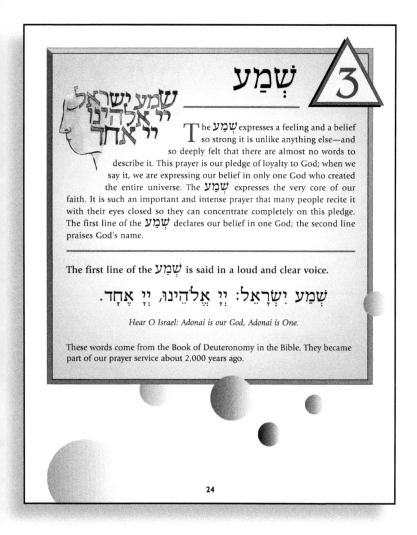

The שְׁמַע expresses a feeling and a belief so strong it is unlike anything else—and so deeply felt that there are almost no words to describe it. This prayer is our pledge of loyalty to God; when we say it, we are expressing our belief in only one God who created the entire universe. The שְׁמַע expresses the very core of our faith. It is such an important and intense prayer that many people recite it with their eyes closed so they can concentrate completely on this pledge. The first line of the שְׁמַע declares our belief in one God; the second line praises God's name.

The first line of the שְׁמַע is said in a loud and clear voice.

שְׁמַע יִשְׂרָאֵל: יְיָ אֱלֹהֵינוּ, יְיָ אֶחָד.

Hear O Israel: Adonai is our God, Adonai is One.

These words come from the Book of Deuteronomy in the Bible. They became part of our prayer service about 2,000 years ago.

24

For Discussion

When we say the שְׁמַע, we are saying that God is our only God. We worship God alone. We worship no other—not other gods, not wealth, not power, not ourselves, not other human beings—only the one God. This is called monotheism.

Ask students for synonyms for "one." (*only; alone; no other; unique; one-of-a-kind*) List them on the board. Then write the English meaning of the שְׁמַע on the chalkboard:

Hear O Israel: Adonai is our God, Adonai is One.

Ask students to rewrite the English meaning of the שְׁמַע using the synonyms for "one."

Some possibilities are:

Hear O Israel: Adonai is our God, (*only*) Adonai.

Hear O Israel: Adonai is our God, Adonai (*alone*).

Hear O Israel: Adonai is our God, Adonai (*and no other*).

INTO THE TEXT

Call on students to read the introduction to the prayer on page 24.

Insights

- What does the word "core" imply? (*innermost part; center; most important; most fundamental; closest to the truth*)

- What does the phrase "core of our faith" imply? (*the heart of our faith; what we do as a people—the way we worship God, the rituals we follow, the way we dress and protect the Torah—grows outward from our core belief that Adonai is one God; the ethical life we follow is based on God's teaching*)

- At what times might you close your eyes to concentrate better? (*when working out a problem; while thinking of what to say in answer to a question; when praying*)

- Why does closing your eyes by covering them with your hand help you concentrate when reciting the שְׁמַע? (*no distractions; can concentrate on the meaning of the words*)

Call on students to read the שְׁמַע on page 24 in unison. Then call on individual students to read the שְׁמַע.

Ask a student to read the English meaning of the שְׁמַע on page 24. Then read the explanation that follows.

PRAYER DICTIONARY

Word Cards

Display Word Cards 2 and 17–20 in turn and ask students to read each one. Then display the Word Cards in random order in a pocket chart or on the edge of the chalkboard.

Call on students to read the cards that mean or contain:

- God's name (יְיָ)
- every word with a silent letter

(שְׁמַע יִשְׂרָאֵל אֱלֹהֵינוּ אֶחָד)

- the word with שׁ and the word with שׂ

(שְׁמַע יִשְׂרָאֵל)

- the first word of the prayer (שְׁמַע) and the word that concludes the prayer (אֶחָד)

WHAT'S MISSING?

Direct students to complete the dictionary exercise. Call on individual students to read their answers to the class. Review the correct answers.

UNSCRAMBLE THE PRAYER

In this activity students will unscramble the prayer and read its words in the correct order.

Ask students to close their texts. Hand out Word Cards 2, and 17–20, one card to each of five students. Have the five students come to the front of the class and arrange themselves in the correct order of the שְׁמַע—right to left. One word will be missing. As they place themselves in the correct order, direct the five students to leave a space where that word would be. Ask the class what the missing word is. (יְיָ) Call on the class to recite the prayer including the missing word.

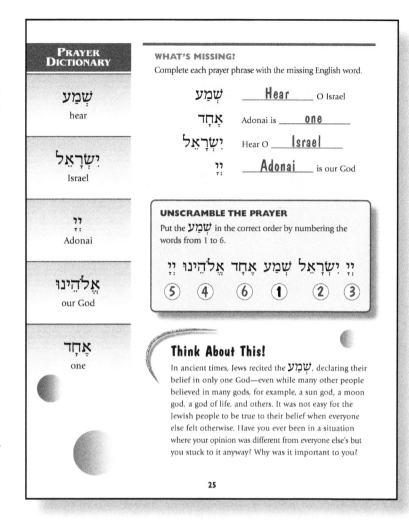

THINK ABOUT THIS!

Discuss as a class responses to the questions at the bottom of the textbook page.

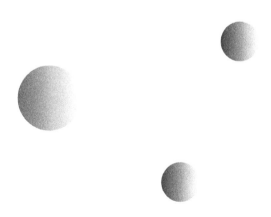

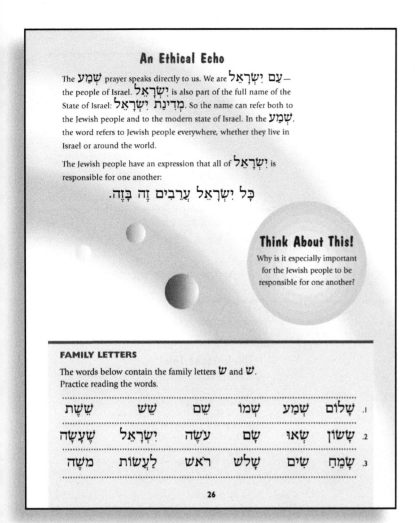

An Ethical Echo

The שְׁמַע prayer speaks directly to us. We are עַם יִשְׂרָאֵל—the people of Israel. יִשְׂרָאֵל is also part of the full name of the State of Israel: מְדִינַת יִשְׂרָאֵל. So the name can refer both to the Jewish people and to the modern state of Israel. In the שְׁמַע, the word refers to Jewish people everywhere, whether they live in Israel or around the world.

The Jewish people have an expression that all of יִשְׂרָאֵל is responsible for one another:

כָּל יִשְׂרָאֵל עֲרֵבִים זֶה בָּזֶה.

Think About This!

Why is it especially important for the Jewish people to be responsible for one another?

FAMILY LETTERS

The words below contain the family letters שׁ and שׂ. Practice reading the words.

שֶׁשֶׁת	שֵׁשׁ	שֵׁם	שְׁמוֹ	שְׁמַע	שָׁלוֹם	.1
שֶׁעָשָׂה	יִשְׂרָאֵל	עָשָׂה	שָׂם	שְׂאוּ	שָׂשׂוֹן	.2
מֹשֶׁה	לַעֲשׂוֹת	רֹאשׁ	שָׁלֹשׁ	שִׂים	שָׂמַח	.3

26

AN ETHICAL ECHO

Read this section together with the students. Which phrase tells us the prayer speaks directly to us? (Hear O Israel—שְׁמַע יִשְׂרָאֵל)

THINK ABOUT THIS!

Read and discuss the question as an extension of the "Ethical Echo." (we are all members of one Jewish family—עַם יִשְׂרָאֵל—and family members take care of one another; Jews in various parts of the world have often lived under oppression, and the ones who could be counted on to take care of their needs were other Jews who understood that all of Israel is responsible for one another; by taking care of one another we have preserved our communities and our people)

For Discussion

In what specific ways do we actively show our responsibility for one another? Encourage students to use specific examples from their own community as well as broader concepts of Jewish responsibility, e.g., visiting the sick (בִּקוּר חוֹלִים), honoring the elderly (כִּבּוּד זְקֵנִים), freeing the captives (פִּדְיוֹן שְׁבוּיִים).

FAMILY LETTERS

Write the letters שׁ and שׂ on the chalkboard. How does the sound of these family members change when the dot moves from one side of the letter to the other side?

Write many examples of שׁ and שׂ on the chalkboard, but draw an open circle in the place of the dot over each letter. Call on students individually to come to the board and write the correct sound ("sh" or "s") inside the circles.

Reading Skills

Double-Duty Dot

Review with students the double-duty dot. The dot can identify the letter שׁ and at the same time serve as the vowel for the preceding letter. Or, the dot can identify the letter שׂ and at the same time serve as the vowel for the שׂ. (Direct students to page 20 of the textbook for review.)

Double Dots

Sometimes שׁ or שׂ looks like this: שֳׁ. If שׁ is at the *beginning* of a word, the letter is a שׁ and the dot on the left is the vowel for the שׂ. (שְׁמַע) But, if שׂ is in the *middle* of a word, the letter is usually a שׂ and the dot on the right is the vowel for the preceding letter (נָשָׂא).

PRAYER BUILDING BLOCKS

Word Endings

A *suffix* is a letter or group of letters that is attached to the end of a word. Every suffix has a specific meaning. Write the suffix נוּ—meaning "us," "our," or "we"—on the chalkboard. Explain to the students that this suffix is attached to many Hebrew words in the siddur. Sometimes, when it is added, the form of the original word changes.

מֶלֶךְ (Ruler)   גּוֹאֵל (Redeemer)

מַלְכֵּנוּ (our Ruler)   גּוֹאֲלֵנוּ (our Redeemer)

READING PRACTICE

Reinforce reading skills before calling on students to read complete lines from the textbook. Ask students to read:

- words with שׁ or שׂ

- words with נוּ endings

- words with a *dagesh* (a dot in the middle of the letter)

- the word on line 2 built on the root meaning "bless" or "praise" (בָּרֵךְ)

אֱלֹהֵינוּ "our God"

The word אֱלֹהֵינוּ is made up of two parts:

אֱלֹהֵי means "God of."

נוּ is an ending that means "us" or "our."

אֱלֹהֵינוּ means "our God."

Circle the Hebrew word that means "our God" in the following prayer:

שְׁמַע יִשְׂרָאֵל: יְיָ (אֱלֹהֵינוּ) יְיָ אֶחָד.

Write the ending that means "us" or "our." _____ נוּ

Write the Hebrew word that means "our God." _____ אֱלֹהֵינוּ

Because our ancestors were the first to know that God is the One God of all the world, we feel especially close to God—and so we say "*our God.*"

READING PRACTICE

Practice reading the following סִדּוּר phrases.

Circle the word אֱלֹהֵינוּ wherever it appears.

1. רְצֵה יְיָ (אֱלֹהֵינוּ) בְּעַמְּךָ יִשְׂרָאֵל.

2. בָּרֵךְ עָלֵינוּ, יְיָ (אֱלֹהֵינוּ) אֶת הַשָּׁנָה הַזֹּאת.

3. אַהֲבָה רַבָּה אֲהַבְתָּנוּ, יְיָ (אֱלֹהֵינוּ)

4. הַשְׁכִּיבֵנוּ יְיָ (אֱלֹהֵינוּ) לְשָׁלוֹם.

In each of the sentences above, the Hebrew word for Adonai also appears. Write the Hebrew word for Adonai. _____ יְיָ

27

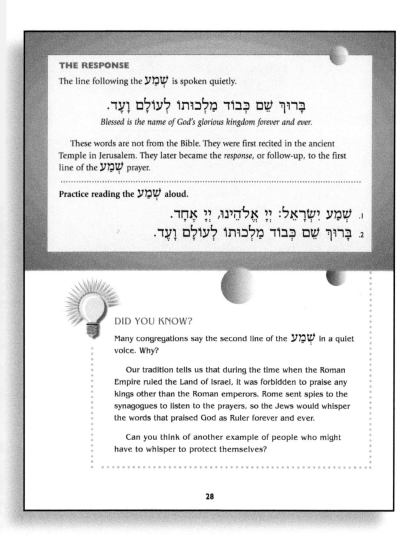

THE RESPONSE

The line following the שְׁמַע is spoken quietly.

בָּרוּךְ שֵׁם כְּבוֹד מַלְכוּתוֹ לְעוֹלָם וָעֶד.

Blessed is the name of God's glorious kingdom forever and ever.

These words are not from the Bible. They were first recited in the ancient Temple in Jerusalem. They later became the *response*, or follow-up, to the first line of the שְׁמַע prayer.

Practice reading the שְׁמַע aloud.

1. שְׁמַע יִשְׂרָאֵל: יְיָ אֱלֹהֵינוּ, יְיָ אֶחָד.
2. בָּרוּךְ שֵׁם כְּבוֹד מַלְכוּתוֹ לְעוֹלָם וָעֶד.

DID YOU KNOW?

Many congregations say the second line of the שְׁמַע in a quiet voice. Why?

Our tradition tells us that during the time when the Roman Empire ruled the Land of Israel, it was forbidden to praise any kings other than the Roman emperors. Rome sent spies to the synagogues to listen to the prayers, so the Jews would whisper the words that praised God as Ruler forever and ever.

Can you think of another example of people who might have to whisper to protect themselves?

28

THE RESPONSE

Write the word "Ruler" with a capital "R" on the chalkboard. Ask the students: What words come to mind when seeing this word with a capital "R"? (*commander, lawgiver, king, queen*) Ask them: What is the role of a Ruler? (*gives us rules or laws to live by; governs our lives*)

Explain to your students that in the second sentence of the שְׁמַע we state our acceptance of Adonai as Israel's eternal Ruler. Direct the students to the top of page 28 of the textbook. Ask them to read the Hebrew sentence following the שְׁמַע and the English meaning of the sentence. What phrase indicates that God is our eternal Ruler "forever and ever"? (לְעוֹלָם וָעֶד)

Call on students to read the explanation of the second line of the שְׁמַע ("These words . . . prayer"). Ask the students to recite this line quietly, in unison.

Divide the class in half. Ask one half to recite the first line of the שְׁמַע. Then, ask the other half to *quietly* recite the second line of the שְׁמַע. Then switch: Ask the second group to read the first line, and the first group to read the second line. If it is the custom in your synagogue, you may wish to ask students to close their eyes.

DID YOU KNOW?

Direct the class to read this section quietly to themselves. Then, ask the following:

• Why do you think the Roman emperors did not allow people to praise anyone except the emperor? (*they saw themselves as the supreme rulers*)

• Why do you think Jews continued to praise God and risk their lives, even when facing these edicts from the emperor? (*they believed in God as the only and the supreme Ruler*)

PRAYER DICTIONARY

Select a student to read each Hebrew word in the Prayer Dictionary. Direct the class to respond in unison with its English meaning. Then reverse and have the student read each English word and have the class respond with the Hebrew.

Place Word Cards 4–5 and 21–23 in random order in a pocket chart or on the edge of the chalkboard. Call on students to read:

- the word built on the root meaning "blessed" or "praised" (בָּרוּךְ)

- the phrase meaning "forever and ever" (לְעוֹלָם וָעֶד)

- the word meaning "name" (שֵׁם)

- the words meaning "the glory of God's kingdom" (כְּבוֹד מַלְכוּתוֹ)

WHAT'S MISSING?

Display Word Cards 4–5 and 21–23. Challenge students to test themselves by covering the Prayer Dictionary in their texts as they complete the answers in "What's Missing?" Invite the students to use the Word Cards to help select the missing words. Then, ask students to uncover the Prayer Dictionary to self-check their answers.

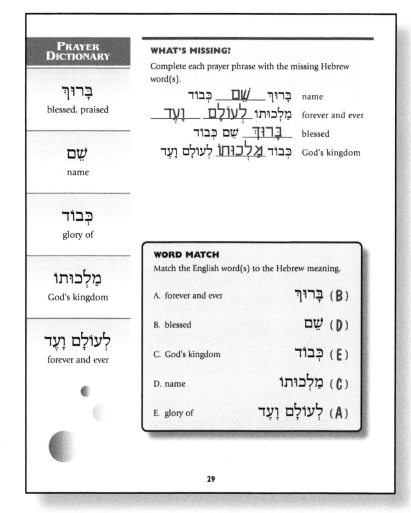

WORD MATCH

Ask students to complete the "Word Match" individually. Challenge them to test themselves by again covering the Prayer Dictionary as they complete the answers in the "Word Match." Then, ask them to uncover the Prayer Dictionary to self-check their answers.

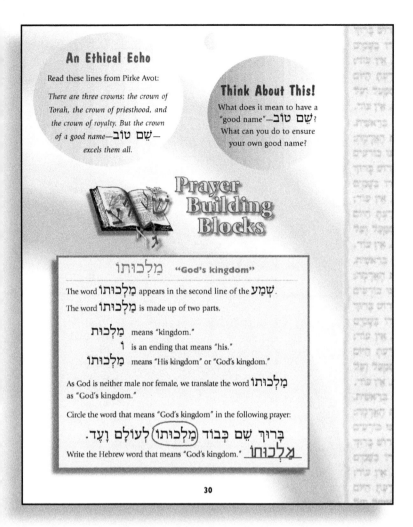

PRAYER BUILDING BLOCKS

Complete this section together with the class.

Create a class chart of "Word Endings." Begin with נוּ ("us," "our," "we"), and וֹ ("his"). Post it on a wall or bulletin board and keep it updated.

AN ETHICAL ECHO

Read the Ethical Echo together with the students. Explain that Pirke Avot means "Ethics of the Fathers" or "Chapters of the Fathers." They are sayings of great rabbis and teachers of about 2,000 years ago. They are part of the Mishnah—a compilation of laws and commentaries on Torah.

Write the following question on the chalkboard: Why does the crown of a good name excel them all? Tell students to come back to this question after discussing the two questions in "Think About This!"

THINK ABOUT THIS!

- What does it mean to have a "good name"—שֵׁם טוֹב? *(to have a good reputation; to be respected; to have people feel good when they hear your name)*

- What can you do to ensure your own good name? *(be kind, thoughtful, respectful of others' needs and feelings, and helpful; don't gossip; perform acts of loving-kindness; conduct one's life with honor)*

Return to the question on the chalkboard: Why does the crown of a good name excel them all? *(a good name comes from acts of worship, tzedakah, and loving-kindness, which exceed mere book learning or priestly status; none of the three crowns is as important as being the kind of person who will earn a good name; Torah represents teaching and learning, but without action one cannot bring honor to Torah, to God, or to oneself)*

The Crown of a Good Name

Create four crowns for a bulletin board display. Label the crowns: Torah, Priesthood, Royalty, and "A Good Name—שֵׁם טוֹב." Have your students create a page of small crowns with their names on them. Each time a student brings honor to his or her name, have the student cut out a crown and place it on the bulletin board under the crown labelled "A Good Name—שֵׁם טוֹב." Ask any student who posts a crown to share the reason for it with the class. (You can set aside a few minutes at the beginning of selected classes to update your שֵׁם טוֹב bulletin board.)

Note: Also see Family Education: "Preparation for Name Day" and "As a Family: Name Day" at the back of this guide.

ROOTS

Review the family letters כ ב ך. Review the definition of a root. (Direct students to page 9 of the textbook for a review, if necessary.) Write the root מ ל כ ("rule") on the board.

List the following words:

מַלְכֵּנוּ

מַלְכוּת

מֶלֶךְ

All three have the same root letters. In which two words does the root letter כ change to another family letter? (מַלְכֵּנוּ   מֶלֶךְ)

Read the section with students. Allow a few minutes for students to circle the root letters in the five words that conclude the exercise.

Call on a student to:

- read the names of the root letters in the first word aloud (*mem, lamed, chaf*)

- read the word (מֶלֶךְ)

Repeat the procedure for each word.

The Fruit of the Tree

Create a fruit tree with three roots from oaktag. Write the letters מ ל כ on the three roots—one letter on each root. Write the meaning—"rule"—on the trunk of the tree. Choose a new type of fruit for this tree and create fruit for it, one piece of fruit for each of the six words built on the root.

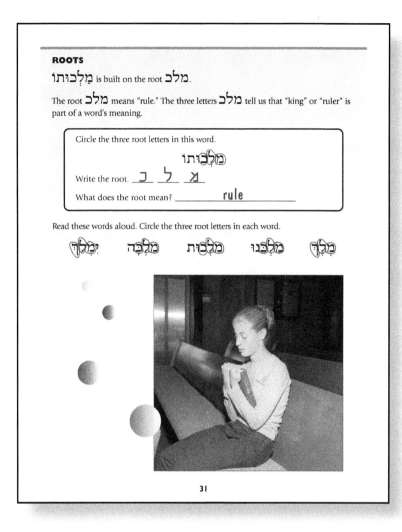

Photo Op

What do you see in the girl's position that conveys a sense of concentration as she recites the שְׁמַע? (*eyes closed, head bowed, embracing the siddur*)

Extending the Opportunity

In the sanctuary or in the classroom, ask students to close their eyes. Encourage them to use their own body language—like that of the girl in the photograph—to convey a sense of concentration. Then recite the שְׁמַע together.

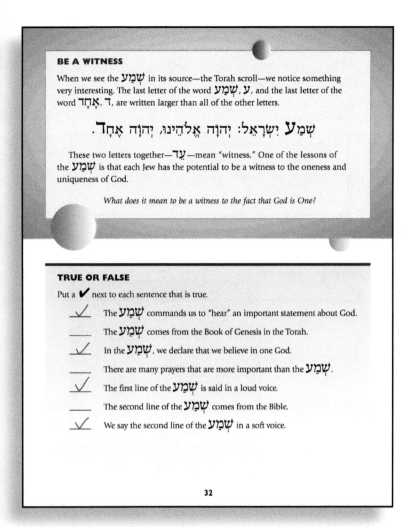

BE A WITNESS

Read the section together with the students. Encourage them to share ideas in response to the question, "What does it mean to be a witness to the fact that God is One?" (*to publicly proclaim that God is One; to believe that God is One; to act as if God is One; to act according to God's teachings*)

A Visit to the Sanctuary

Visit the sanctuary with your students; arrange in advance to have the Torah scroll open to the שְׁמַע. Allow each student to see how the sentence appears in the *Sefer Torah*—the Torah Scroll. Ask each student to read the sentence directly from the *Sefer Torah* using a *yad* to point to each word.

After each student has had a chance to read the שְׁמַע, ask them the following questions:

* What is the significance of pointing to each word when we read Torah? (*each and every word is important; we emphasize each word of God's teaching; by looking closely at each word we learn more about the meaning of the Torah*)

* Why do we use a *yad*? (*to preserve the scroll from damage; to show our respect for the Torah*)

TRUE OR FALSE

When reviewing students' answers, after identifying the false statements, call upon individual students to change the false statements so that they become correct.

(*#2—Book of Deuteronomy; #4—no prayers are more important than the שְׁמַע; #6—the words are not from the Bible, they were first said in the ancient Temple*)

FLUENT READING

Reading Skills: Sh'va with a Double Letter

Explain to your students: sometimes the same letter appears twice consecutively in a word. If the first letter has a sh'va (ְ) the sh'va is sounded as "uh."

Write these words on the chalkboard in this way:

הַ לְלוּ   רוֹ מְמוּ   הִ נְנִי

Ask a student to come to the board and circle all of the double letters. (נְנ   מְמ   לְל)

Then, ask the students to (1) pronounce the blended (circled) letters, (2) read the whole words containing the circled letters, and (3) read the whole line.

Selected Reading

Direct students to "Fluent Reading" on page 33. Call on students to read:

- the word in line 3 with double letters (הַלְלוּ)

- the word in line 2 built on the root meaning "rule" (מַלְכוּתוֹ)

- the words in lines 1, 9, and 10 with word endings meaning "us," "our," or "we" (נוּ ending)

- the words in lines 1–8 with שׁ or שׂ

Strike 12!

To play this game, draw a clock on the chalkboard and write the numeral 12 in the 12 o'clock position. In place of the other numbers, write random Hebrew letters found in Fluent Reading. Ask a student to select a letter on the clock and to read a word from "Fluent Reading" that contains the letter. Then, ask the student to erase the letter on the clock and replace it with the proper number. For example: A student might select the letter ע which you have placed at the 5:00 position. The student should read a word with ע in it (such as עֶרֶב on line 11). Then the student should erase the ע and replace it with the number 5. A second student then selects another letter and continues in the same way. The game is over when all the letters have been replaced by numbers and the clock strikes 12!

FLUENT READING

Practice reading the lines below.

1. שְׁמַע יִשְׂרָאֵל: יְיָ אֱלֹהֵינוּ, יְיָ אֶחָד.

2. בָּרוּךְ שֵׁם כְּבוֹד מַלְכוּתוֹ לְעוֹלָם וָעֶד.

3. הַלְלוּ, עַבְדֵי יְיָ, הַלְלוּ אֶת שֵׁם יְיָ.

4. וְהוּא אֶחָד, וְאֵין שֵׁנִי.

5. בַּיּוֹם הַהוּא יִהְיֶה יְיָ אֶחָד וּשְׁמוֹ אֶחָד.

6. לֹא תִשָּׂא אֶת שֵׁם יְהֹוָה אֱלֹהֶיךָ לַשָּׁוְא.

7. צוּר יִשְׂרָאֵל, קוּמָה בְּעֶזְרַת יִשְׂרָאֵל.

8. שְׁמַע! בַּיָּמִים הָהֵם בַּזְּמַן הַזֶּה.

9. וְטוֹב וְיָפֶה הַדָּבָר הַזֶּה עָלֵינוּ לְעוֹלָם וָעֶד.

10. אַהֲבָה רַבָּה אֲהַבְתָּנוּ, יְיָ אֱלֹהֵינוּ.

11. וַיְהִי עֶרֶב וַיְהִי בֹקֶר, יוֹם אֶחָד.

33

Variation

To provide additional reading practice, ask the students to read the word and then the complete line before replacing the letter with a number on the clock.

WORKSHEET

Hand out copies of the worksheet for Lesson 3 for a review of the vocabulary and the concepts underlying the שְׁמַע.

FAMILY EDUCATION

Read the suggested Family Education "Preparation for Name Day" event description. The page "As a Family: Name Day" is used in conjunction with the Name Day event. The "As a Family" activity page can also be photocopied and used independently. Both pages are located at the back of this guide.

Name: _____

שְׁמַע

1. Write the words of the שְׁמַע in the correct order.

יְיָ   שְׁמַע   אֶחָד   אֱלֹהֵינוּ   יְיָ   יִשְׂרָאֵל

_____

Unscramble the phrases to write the English meaning of the שְׁמַע prayer.

Hear O Israel   Adonai is One   Adonai is our God

_____

_____

2. In the Torah, the last letter in the first word and in the last word of the שְׁמַע are larger than the other letters.

שְׁמַע   אֶחָד

What is the English meaning of the word עֵד? _____

3. Why is the word עֵד so important in understanding the meaning of the שְׁמַע?

_____

4. Who is יִשְׂרָאֵל? _____

   What is יִשְׂרָאֵל? _____

5. Write the words of the second sentence of the שְׁמַע in the correct order.

מַלְכוּתוֹ   בָּרוּךְ   וָעֶד   שֵׁם   לְעוֹלָם   כְּבוֹד

_____

_____

Unscramble the phrases to write the English meaning of the second sentence.

of God's glorious kingdom   forever and ever   blessed is the name

_____

LESSON 4 וְאָהַבְתָּ

LEARNING OBJECTIVES

Prayer Reading Skills

Prefix: הַ ("the")

Root: א ה ב ("love")

Word endings: ךָ ("you," "your")

וֹ = ָ

Prayer Concepts

Reciprocal love between the Jewish people and God

Significance of the mezuzah as a reminder of our love for God and our respect for God's commandments

Ethical Echo: *Talmud Torah*

BEYOND THE TEXTBOOK

Letter ו with dot over it (וֹ)

Double *sh'va*

Prefixes: וּ, וְ ("and")

Suffix: כֶם ("you," "your"—plural)

ABOUT THE PRAYER

The וְאָהַבְתָּ comes directly from the Torah (Deuteronomy 6:5–9). It follows immediately after the שְׁמַע in the Torah and in the siddur. The passage commands each person to demonstrate love for God "with all your heart, and with all your soul, and with all your might." We are commanded to place a mezuzah on the doorposts of our homes as a constant reminder of our love for God and our respect for God's commandments.

INSTRUCTIONAL MATERIALS

Text pages 34–41

Word Cards 24–29

Worksheet for Lesson 4

Family Education: "As a Family: Showing Love" (at the back of this guide)

SET INDUCTION

Write the following headings on the chalkboard:

- How your parents show love for you
- How you show love for your parents

Ask students to contribute suggestions for each heading, and write their responses on the chalkboard. Encourage students to give specific answers, not generalities. *(Parents' love for you: giving hugs and kisses; providing food, clothing, shelter; taking care of your health; creating fun times and experiences. Your love for parents: giving hugs and kisses; showing respect; helping with chores; remembering birthdays; reflecting parents' values.)*

Introduce the term "reciprocal love." Discuss the meaning of the word "reciprocal." *(mutual; back and forth; giving and getting at the same time)*

Ask the students:

- How do our lists reflect the fact that there is reciprocal love in your home? *(parents and children are doing things for each other)*

- What does reciprocal love tell us about the commitment in your home? *(concern and caring for each other; valuing each other; showing respect for one another; desire for harmony and peace in the home)*

וְאָהַבְתָּ 4

How do you show your parents that you love them? You might bring Dad breakfast in bed or help Mom weed the garden. Another important way to demonstrate your love for your parents is to show respect for them. The וְאָהַבְתָּ prayer reminds us to love God by respecting and following God's commandments. We put a mezuzah—a small box containing the words of the שְׁמַע and וְאָהַבְתָּ—on the doorposts of our house. Each time we look at the mezuzah it reminds us of our love for God and of our respect for God's commandments.

וְאָהַבְתָּ comes immediately after the שְׁמַע in the siddur.

Practice reading the וְאָהַבְתָּ.

1. וְאָהַבְתָּ אֵת יְיָ אֱלֹהֶיךָ
2. בְּכָל-לְבָבְךָ וּבְכָל-נַפְשְׁךָ וּבְכָל-מְאֹדֶךָ.
3. וְהָיוּ הַדְּבָרִים הָאֵלֶּה, אֲשֶׁר אָנֹכִי מְצַוְּךָ הַיּוֹם, עַל-לְבָבֶךָ.
4. וְשִׁנַּנְתָּם לְבָנֶיךָ, וְדִבַּרְתָּ בָּם בְּשִׁבְתְּךָ בְּבֵיתֶךָ,
5. וּבְלֶכְתְּךָ בַדֶּרֶךְ, וּבְשָׁכְבְּךָ וּבְקוּמֶךָ.
6. וּקְשַׁרְתָּם לְאוֹת עַל-יָדֶךָ, וְהָיוּ לְטֹטָפֹת בֵּין עֵינֶיךָ.
7. וּכְתַבְתָּם עַל-מְזֻזוֹת בֵּיתֶךָ וּבִשְׁעָרֶיךָ.

You shall love Adonai, your God,
with all your heart, and with all your soul, and with all your might.
Set these words, which I command you this day, upon your heart.
Teach them to your children, and speak of them when you are at home,
and when you go on your way, and when you lie down, and when you get up.
Bind them as a sign upon your hand and let them be symbols between your eyes.
Write them on the doorposts of your house and on your gates.

34

Reading Chain

Direct students to the וְאָהַבְתָּ prayer on page 34. Select a student to be the first reader to start the chain.

- Ask this student to read line 1 to the person on the right.

- Then ask the second student to read line 2 to the student on his or her right.

- Have the students continue reading in turn around the room, thereby creating a "reading chain."

- Continue the reading chain so that all students have an opportunity to read a line. If you reach the end of the וְאָהַבְתָּ prayer before all students have had a turn, then start it over again.

Variation: Read phrase by phrase instead of line by line.

INTO THE TEXT

Read the introduction on the top of page 34 with students.

Basic מְזוּזָה Facts

- The word מְזוּזָה means "doorpost" (plural מְזוּזוֹת). The concluding sentence in the וְאָהַבְתָּ tells us to "write these words [of the וְאָהַבְתָּ and שְׁמַע] on the doorposts of your house." Over time, the parchment on which the וְאָהַבְתָּ is written as well as the case that holds and protects it came to be called the מְזוּזָה. Traditionally, מְזוּזוֹת are placed on the doorpost leading into the home and on the doorposts of each room in the home (except for bathrooms and storerooms).

- On many מְזוּזוֹת, facing outward, is God's name (שַׁדַּי—usually translated as "Almighty") or the letter שׁ. The most common explanation for this is that the Hebrew letters that make up the name שַׁדַּי are the initials—the acronym —שׁוֹמֵר דַּלְתוֹת יִשְׂרָאֵל— for the phrase "guardian/protector of the doors of Israel."

- The מְזוּזָה is placed on the right-hand doorpost as one faces into the home or room. It is placed in a diagonal position with the top portion pointing inward. It is placed at the beginning of the upper third of the doorpost.

For Discussion

Why was this place and this angle chosen? (*a compromise between those rabbis who felt it should be straight up and those who felt it should be horizontal; other possible answers: we symbolically look upward toward God and Torah, the right side indicates the right way to lead our lives, the name שַׁדַּי or the letter שׁ can be easily seen at this angle*)

We say a blessing when we attach a מְזוּזָה.

בָּרוּךְ אַתָּה, יְיָ אֱלֹהֵינוּ, מֶלֶךְ הָעוֹלָם
אֲשֶׁר קִדְּשָׁנוּ בְּמִצְוֹתָיו וְצִוָּנוּ לִקְבֹּעַ מְזוּזָה.

Praised are You, Adonai our God, Ruler of the world, who makes us holy with commandments and commands us to attach a mezuzah.

Suggestion: Invite parents to a mezuzah ceremony in which you affix a mezuzah to your classroom door. Say the blessing together.

PRAYER DICTIONARY

Word Cards

Display Word Cards 24–29.

Ask students to select the word(s) that:

- means "doorposts" (מְזֻזוֹת)
- end with letter *tav* (וְאָהַבְתָּ לְאוֹת מְזֻזוֹת)
- have a final letter (הַדְּבָרִים לְבָבְךָ בֵּיתֶךָ)

Playing Concentration

Ask students to read each word on the Word Cards in unison. After they read each word, show them or read them the English meaning on the back of the Word Card. Repeat two more times.

Next, write the English meaning of each word on the chalkboard, and post the Word Cards on to the board in random order. (You can use tape or Fun-Tac.)

Divide the class into 3 or 4 teams. Give each team a turn to place the Word Cards next to the proper English meaning on the board. Team members should work together to make their "concentrated" decisions. After each team is done, again place the Word Cards in random order back on the board. The team gets one point for each correct match.

Top Score: 6 points

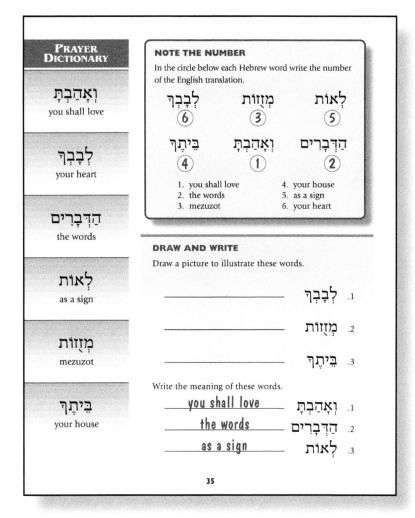

Reading Practice

Ask students to locate individual Prayer Dictionary words in the prayer on page 34. After a student identifies a word and its location (for example, הַדְּבָרִים—line 3, second word) have the class read the whole line aloud in unison. Then ask the student who located the word to read the line individually.

Climb the Steps

Draw a series of 13 steps on the chalkboard and number them 1–13. Ask each student to climb the steps by reading each of the 13 words with the prefix meaning "and" (וְ or וּ) in the וְאָהַבְתָּ. Allow students time beforehand to identify and circle the words.

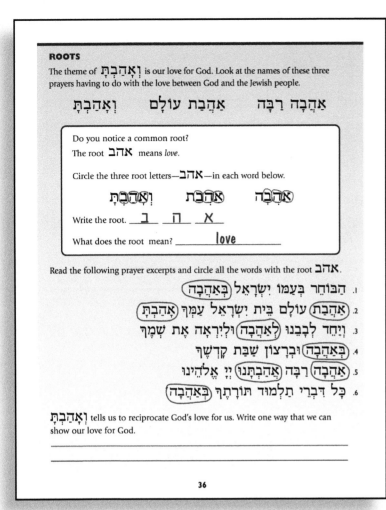

The Fruit of the Tree

Create another fruit tree with three roots from oaktag. Write the letters א ה ב on the roots—one letter on each root. Write the meaning of the root—"love"—on the trunk of the tree. Create fruit for the tree (a type of fruit you haven't used before)—one piece of fruit for each of the root words found on the page.

ROOTS

Read the introductory sentence aloud with students. Call on individual students to read the names of the three prayers:

וְאָהַבְתָּ   אַהֲבַת עוֹלָם   אַהֲבָה רַבָּה

Ask the students to complete this first section of "Roots." Then ask them to return to page 21 in their textbooks. Review the "Think About This!" question and "Second Blessing Before the Shema," to remind students of the relationship between these blessings and the וְאָהַבְתָּ.

Direct students to page 36, Hebrew lines 1–6. Ask them to circle the words built on the root א ה ב. Call on individuals to read each circled word aloud.

Reading Teams

Students count off to form reading teams of two: א-ב, א ב, א ב. Assign each א-ב team either the odd numbered lines (1, 3, and 5) or the even numbered lines (2, 4, and 6) on page 36 to practice. Call on the teams to read their lines aloud in the following manner:

- Partner א should read the line but stop immediately before each circled א ה ב word. Partner ב should step in to read the circled א ה ב word(s). Then, partner א should resume reading.

- The two partners should then read each assigned line aloud together.

After the reading exercise, ask the partners to meet again to discuss the statement at the bottom of the page. Call on teams to share their insights with the class. (*observe Shabbat; observe holidays; recite Shema; perform acts of loving-kindness; give tzedakah; preserve the earth*)

PRAYER BUILDING BLOCKS

הַדְּבָרִים "the words"

Explain to the class that the prefixes הַ and הָ mean "the." Read and complete the "Prayer Building Blocks" with students. Then direct the class to page 34 of the textbook, line 3, and ask them to read:

- the Hebrew sentence (line 3) in unison

- the English meaning in unison. ("Set these words . . . your heart")

Then, ask individual students to read line 3 again.

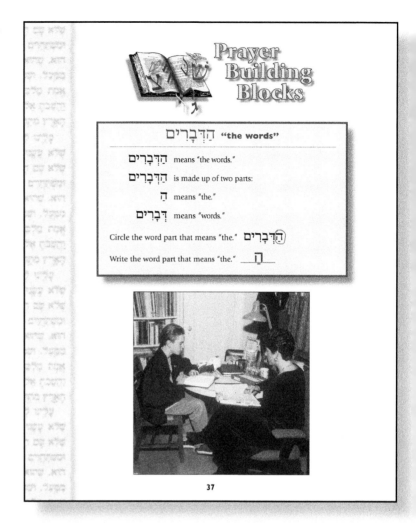

Prayer Building Blocks

הַדְּבָרִים "the words"

הַדְּבָרִים	means "the words."
הַדְּבָרִים	is made up of two parts:
הַ	means "the."
דְּבָרִים	means "words."

Circle the word part that means "the." הַ‍דְּבָרִים

Write the word part that means "the." ___ הַ

37

Photo Op

Direct students to the English translation of וְאָהַבְתָּ on page 34. Ask them to compare that text with the photo on page 37. Which phrases in the prayer are depicted in the photo? (*teach them to your children, and speak of them when you are at home*) Call on individual students to locate and read the Hebrew phrases with this meaning (line 4).

Ask the class:

- What are we to teach to our children and speak of when at home? (*the words of the* שְׁמַע *and the* וְאָהַבְתָּ *as well as all of Torah*)

- Why is this *our* responsibility? (*we are commanded to pass down our belief in one God and our heritage from generation to generation*)

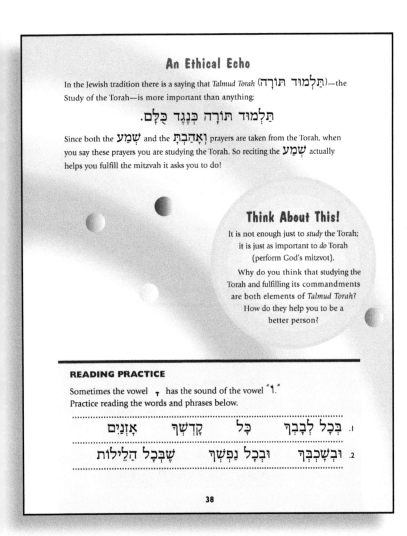

An Ethical Echo

In the Jewish tradition there is a saying that *Talmud Torah* (תַּלְמוּד תּוֹרָה)—the Study of the Torah—is more important than anything:

תַּלְמוּד תּוֹרָה כְּנֶגֶד כֻּלָם.

Since both the שְׁמַע and the וְאָהַבְתָּ prayers are taken from the Torah, when you say these prayers you are studying the Torah. So reciting the שְׁמַע actually helps you fulfill the mitzvah it asks you to do!

Think About This!

It is not enough just to *study* the Torah; it is just as important to *do* Torah (perform God's mitzvot).

Why do you think that studying the Torah and fulfilling its commandments are both elements of *Talmud Torah*? How do they help you to be a better person?

READING PRACTICE

Sometimes the vowel ָ has the sound of the vowel "וֹ."
Practice reading the words and phrases below.

1. אָזְנַיִם   קָדְשֶׁךָ   כָּל   בְּכָל לְבָבְךָ

2. וּבְשָׁכְבְּךָ   וּבְכָל נַפְשְׁךָ   שֶׁבְּכָל הַלֵּילוֹת

38

AN ETHICAL ECHO

Read the section aloud. Review the meaning of the word "mitzvah." (*commandment*) Direct students to the וְאָהַבְתָּ on page 34, and ask them to review the English meaning of the passage. Which sentence commands us to study Torah? (*sentence 3: lines 4–5*)

Ask students to read the English meaning aloud in unison. ("Teach them . . . and when you get up.") Then have students read the Hebrew sentence aloud, in unison and individually. (*sentence 3: lines 4–5*)

THINK ABOUT THIS!

Read and discuss the two questions that conclude the section. (*studying helps provide an understanding of the commandments; studying brings us to a new level of awareness; fulfilling the commandments reinforces Jewish tradition, betters the lives of others, protects the earth*)

READING PRACTICE

Ask a student to read the first phrase and then to call on another student to read the next word or phrase. The second student then chooses a third, and so on. Remind students to carefully pronounce the vowel sounds as they read each word.

PRAYER BUILDING BLOCKS

Read the explanation of בֵּיתְךָ with students. Have students complete the questions following the prayer. Call on students to read the circled words aloud:

- Ask one student to be the "Reader." Ask the Reader to read each word aloud, stopping each time before the word ending ךָ. Then ask the class to read the word ending ךָ in unison. Repeat several times. Each time ask a different student to be the Reader.

- Divide the class into two-person reading partnerships. Ask each partnership to read aloud following the same procedure described above.

Add the word ending ךָ to your class "Word Endings" chart (see Lesson 3 of this guide).

Study Partners

Create study partnerships for the first three lines of the וְאָהַבְתָּ by dividing your class randomly into three groups of roughly equal size. Assign one group to each of the three sentences.

- Ask each study partnership to mark off its Hebrew and English sentence with a highlighter or pencil.

- Ask each partnership to practice reading their sentence aloud. Make sure they help each other with pronunciation and fluency.

- Ask each to also discuss the meaning of the assigned English sentence, and to be prepared to explain it in their own words.

When the partnerships are prepared, ask them to read their sentences to the class, and to explain the English meaning of each sentence.

Teach students how to chant the וְאָהַבְתָּ.

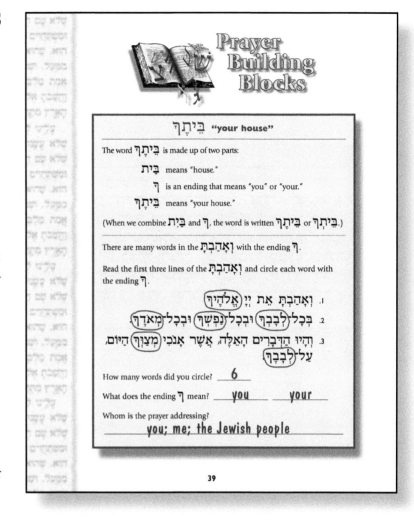

BACK TO THE SOURCES

> **BACK TO THE SOURCES**
>
> This is a page from the Book of Deuteronomy. In this selection Moses talks to the Children of Israel about how they should behave when they enter the land of Canaan.
>
> Can you find and read the שְׁמַע?
>
> Can you find and read the וְאָהַבְתָּ?
>
> Can you find the two larger letters (עד)? What do they mean when combined to form one word?
>
> ד שְׁמַע יִשְׂרָאֵל יְהוָֹה אֱלֹהֵינוּ יְהוָֹה ׀ אֶחָד: וְאָהַבְתָּ אֵת
> יְהוָֹה אֱלֹהֶיךָ בְּכָל־לְבָבְךָ וּבְכָל־נַפְשְׁךָ וּבְכָל־מְאֹדֶךָ: ה
> וְהָיוּ הַדְּבָרִים הָאֵלֶּה אֲשֶׁר אָנֹכִי מְצַוְּךָ הַיּוֹם עַל־לְבָבֶךָ: ו
> וְשִׁנַּנְתָּם לְבָנֶיךָ וְדִבַּרְתָּ בָּם בְּשִׁבְתְּךָ בְּבֵיתֶךָ וּבְלֶכְתְּךָ ז
> בַדֶּרֶךְ וּבְשָׁכְבְּךָ וּבְקוּמֶךָ: וּקְשַׁרְתָּם לְאוֹת עַל־יָדֶךָ וְהָיוּ ח
> לְטֹטָפֹת בֵּין עֵינֶיךָ: וּכְתַבְתָּם עַל־מְזֻזוֹת בֵּיתֶךָ וּבִשְׁעָרֶיךָ: ט
>
> 40

Explain that this is a page from the *Ḥumash*. It resembles the passage as it appears in the Torah. However, in the *Sefer Torah*—the Torah Scroll—there are only Hebrew letters, while in the *Ḥumash* there are also vowels, *trope* marks, and verses indicated by numerals (1, 2, 3 . . .) or by Hebrew letters which represent numbers.

Direct students' attention to the *trope* marks. They indicate the melody for chanting the words of Torah. Your students will probably learn to chant *trope* when they prepare to become a Bar or Bat Mitzvah.

Read the introduction on page 40 with the students. Call on individual students to respond to the questions which follow the introduction. *(the two large letters, עד, mean "witness"; review the significance of the term "witness" on page 32 in the textbook)*

Bring several copies of the *Ḥumash* to class. Have students locate the שְׁמַע and וְאָהַבְתָּ in Deuteronomy 6:5–9 and read it directly from the *Ḥumash*.

Take students to the sanctuary. Open the *Sefer Torah* to the שְׁמַע and וְאָהַבְתָּ. Now that students have some familiarity with these passages, ask individual students to read directly from the Torah without the assistance of vowels. You might consider also asking a Torah reader in your congregation to chant the שְׁמַע and וְאָהַבְתָּ from the *Sefer Torah*.

FLUENT READING

Read the introduction aloud with students. Then review the following reading skills with the class.

Reading Rule: וֹ vs. וּ

Write the letter ו on the chalkboard. Then, add a dot over the ו to make a וֹ. Ask the students: "What vowel does it resemble?" ("o") Explain that there is a clue that can tell you when וֹ is a *letter* saying "vo" and when it is a *vowel* saying "o." If the letter preceding וֹ already has a vowel, then וֹ is a *letter* with a vowel over it.

Write צַוֹ on the chalkboard. Have students explain why וֹ is a letter with a vowel above it. *(because the letter preceding the וֹ already has a vowel)*

Write on the chalkboard:

מִצְוֹת   מִצְוֹתַי   בְּמִצְוֹתָיו

Call on students to circle צַוֹ in each word. Call on students to read each word. Which word is on line 1 at the top of page 41? (מִצְוֹתַי) Call on students to read the hyphenated word combination (אֶת־כָּל־מִצְוֹתָי).

Direct students to look for and circle the word ending כֶם in lines 2–3 at the top of page 41. The ending כֶם means "you" in plural. Call on individual students to read each word. Now call on students to read the word along with the word that precedes it. Direct students to look for and read the word with a double *sh'va.* (תִּזְכְּרוּ— *line 1, second word, at the top of the page*)

Read the explanation in the middle of the page with students. Then, ask students to count off 1-2-3-4, 1-2-3-4, 1-2-3-4 around the room. Form four groups: all the 1's, all the 2's, all the 3's, and all the 4's. Next, assign group 1 to line 1; group 2 - line 2; group 3 - line 3; group 4 - line 4. Have the groups meet and the group members assist each other as they practice reading the lines. Have groups read the assigned line in unison. Then ask individual members to read the assigned line.

FLUENT READING

Some congregations add these words after the וְאָהַבְתָּ.
Practice reading the lines below.

1. לְמַעַן תִּזְכְּרוּ וַעֲשִׂיתֶם אֶת־כָּל־מִצְוֹתָי, וִהְיִיתֶם קְדֹשִׁים

2. לֵאלֹהֵיכֶם. אֲנִי יְיָ אֱלֹהֵיכֶם, אֲשֶׁר הוֹצֵאתִי אֶתְכֶם מֵאֶרֶץ

3. מִצְרַיִם לִהְיוֹת לָכֶם לֵאלֹהִים. אֲנִי יְיָ אֱלֹהֵיכֶם.

The blessing that follows after the שְׁמַע is called the גְּאֻלָּה—Redemption. It praises God for saving us from slavery in Egypt. You'll learn more about the song at the heart of the גְּאֻלָּה in the next chapter.

Meanwhile, practice reading these lines from the גְּאֻלָּה.

1. אֱמֶת וְיַצִּיב, וְאָהוּב וְחָבִיב, וְנוֹרָא וְאַדִּיר.

2. מִמִּצְרַיִם גְּאַלְתָּנוּ, יְיָ אֱלֹהֵינוּ, וּמִבֵּית עֲבָדִים פְּדִיתָנוּ.

3. תְּהִלּוֹת לְאֵל עֶלְיוֹן, בָּרוּךְ הוּא וּמְבֹרָךְ. מֹשֶׁה וּבְנֵי

4. יִשְׂרָאֵל לְךָ עָנוּ שִׁירָה בְּשִׂמְחָה רַבָּה, וְאָמְרוּ כֻלָּם:

Now turn to Chapter 5 for the song at the heart of the גְּאֻלָּה—מִי כָמֹכָה!

41

WORKSHEET

Hand out copies of the worksheet for Lesson 4 for students to review the order of prayers as well as the concepts in the וְאָהַבְתָּ.

FAMILY EDUCATION

Duplicate and send home with students the Family Education page, "As a Family: Showing Love" at the back of this guide.

Name: _____

וְאָהַבְתָּ

1. Circle the correct word: The וְאָהַבְתָּ comes before/after the שְׁמַע.

2. Unscramble the English letters and write the word below the matching root.

   vole   eneingv   leur   slebs

   מ ל כ   א ה ב   ע ר ב   ב ר כ

   _____   _____   _____   _____

3. Circle the part of the word that means "you" or "your." בֵּיתֶךָ

4. The מְזוּזָה:

   Where do we place a מְזוּזָה?
   _____

   What passages from Torah are inside a מְזוּזָה?
   _____

   What does a מְזוּזָה represent? _____
   _____

5. How has God shown love for us?
   _____

   How do we show our love for God?
   _____
   _____

6. Why are we to teach the words of Torah to our children in each generation?
   _____

LEARNING OBJECTIVES

Prayer Reading Skills

Review root: כ ל מ

Root: ק ד שׁ ("holy")

Prefixes: בְּ, בָּ, בַּ, בִּ ("in," "in the," "among the")

BEYOND THE TEXTBOOK

Review: family letters כ ב

double dots שׁ

letters with no sound א ע ה (at the end of a word)

dagesh that does not change the sound of the letter

Term: שֹׁרֶשׁ ("root")

ABOUT THE PRAYER

The passage מִי כָמֹכָה originates in the Torah (Exodus 15:11). We are told that the Israelites sang this passage while crossing the Sea of Reeds from slavery in Egypt to freedom. We remember this historic event each year at our Passover seder.

The song proclaims God as the Redeemer, the Deliverer, of our people. It recognizes that God delivered the Jewish people from slavery in Egypt; and God brought us safely across the Sea of Reeds to freedom. The song the Israelites sang in praise so many centuries ago has today become part of the morning and evening prayer service. It continues to remind us of our obligation to fulfill the mitzvah of פִּדְיוֹן שְׁבוּיִים—redeeming captives. It concludes by praising God for our redemption —Birkat Ge'ulah.

Ḥanukkah Connection

Echoing this song, Judah Maccabee cried out in battle: מִי כָמֹכָה בָּאֵלִם יְיָ. The name Maccabee is supposedly an acronym based on these four words.

INSTRUCTIONAL MATERIALS

Text pages 42–51

Word Cards 2, 30–34

Worksheet for Lesson 5

Family Education: "As a Family: Crossing the Sea" (at the back of this guide)

SET INDUCTION

In every generation one ought to regard oneself as though personally coming out of Egypt . . . Not only our ancestors did the Holy One, blessed be Adonai, redeem, but also ourselves did Adonai redeem with them. (from the Passover haggadah)

Write the above quotation from the haggadah on the upper portion of the chalkboard or on oaktag and hang it on the wall. Beneath the quotation create the outline of a rectangle as follows:

- Write the seven-letter term "slavery" vertically down the left side of the rectangle.
- Write the seven-letter term "freedom" vertically down the right side of the rectangle.
- Draw a wavy horizontal line—to represent water— across the top, connecting the first letter in each word.
- Draw a wavy horizontal line across the bottom, connecting the last letter in each word.

Write the names of some of those who left Egypt during the Exodus (e.g., Moses, Aaron, Miriam) on the path created by the parted sea—that is, inside the rectangular shape heading away from "slavery" and towards "freedom." Then, call on each student to add his or her own name along with those of our ancestors to symbolically show that it's as if we all personally came out of Egypt.

For Discussion

- Why should we each regard ourselves as though we personally came out of Egypt? *(only by personally remembering slavery and the flight to freedom can we appreciate our lives as a free people and understand the lives of those not yet free)*
- What does freedom for the Jewish people mean to *you? (freedom to engage in Jewish rituals such as Shabbat and holiday observances; freedom to engage in life-cycle rituals such as bar and bat mitzvah; freedom to learn about Judaism, to study Torah; freedom to celebrate our history)*

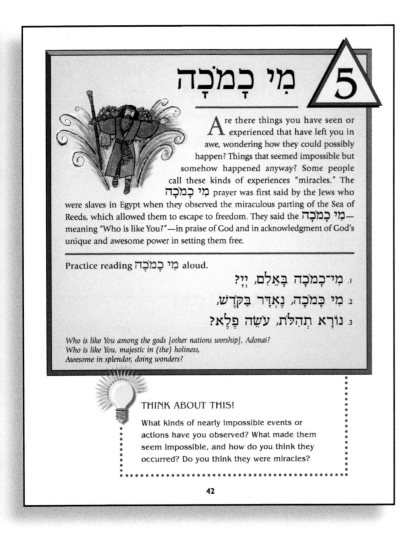

INTO THE TEXT

Have the students read the introduction to the prayer on page 42. Note: The Sea of Reeds (יַם סוּף) is also referred to as the Red Sea.

From the Torah

We read the story of how the Jews left Egypt in the Book of Exodus (13:17–14:31.) The song we sang in celebration of our freedom is found in Exodus 15:1–18. Note: The verses which have become part of the prayer service are Exodus 15:11, 18.

Bring a Ḥumash to class—ideally one per student. Ask students to read aloud in English the account of our coming out of Egypt.

Before reading the Hebrew of the מִי כָמֹכָה prayer from start to finish, review the following reading skills with your students.

Family Letters: כ כֿ

Read aloud the second word in lines 1 and 2.

(כָמֹכָה   כָמֹכָה)

Read aloud the first two words in each line.

(מִי כָמֹכָה   מִי כָמֹכָה)

Double Dots: שׁ

Remind your students of "sho" at the beginning of a word. Write שָׁרֵשׁ on the chalkboard and ask individual students to read it.

Remind your students of "os" in the middle of a word. Write עֹשֵׂה on the chalkboard and ask individual students to read it (see line 3).

Letters with No Sound: א ע ה (at the End of a Word)

Read each word in lines 1–3 that has א, ע, or unsounded ה (found without a vowel at the end of a word).
(כָמֹכָה בָאֵלִם כָמֹכָה נֶאְדָּר נוֹרָא עֹשֵׂה פֶלֶא)

Dagesh That Does Not Change the Sound of the Letter

Read each word in lines 2 and 3 that has a "silent" *dagesh.* (נֶאְדָּר בַּקֹּדֶשׁ תְהִלֹּת)

Reading practice

Ask students to read lines 1–3 in unison. Lead the reading yourself in order to maintain cohesiveness and reinforce pronunciation.

Have the class count off "English-Hebrew-English-Hebrew . . ." (instead of 1-2, 1-2, 1-2 . . .) around the room. Ask the "English" group to read each English line in unison and the "Hebrew" group to respond to each line by reading the corresponding Hebrew. Then switch roles.

PRAYER DICTIONARY

Select a student to read the Hebrew words in the Prayer Dictionary. Ask the class to respond to each Hebrew word with its English meaning. Then select a new student and switch: Ask the reader to read the English and have the class respond with the Hebrew meaning.

Word Cards

Display the Word Cards 2 and 30–32 in random order. Select a student to read aloud the English meaning of line 1 on page 42. Select another student to place the corresponding Hebrew Word Cards in the correct right-to-left order. (מִי כָמֹכָה בָּאֵלִם יְיָ)

Display Word Cards 30, 31, 33, and 34. Select a student to read aloud the English meaning of line 2 on page 42. Select another student to place the corresponding Hebrew Word Cards in the correct right-left order. (מִי כָמֹכָה נֶאְדָּר בַּקֹּדֶשׁ)

SEARCH AND CIRCLE

Direct students to complete this exercise individually. Have them cover the Prayer Dictionary while working on the exercise. Then ask them to uncover the Prayer Dictionary and check their own answers.

Vocabulary Know-How

Challenge students to give the English meaning of each Hebrew word *not* circled in the activity "Search and Circle." *(meanings from right to left: line 1—hear, siddur or prayerbook; line 2—among the gods, who; line 3—Israel, in holiness; line 4—name, one; line 5—among the gods, praise; line 6—forever and ever, who is to be praised)*

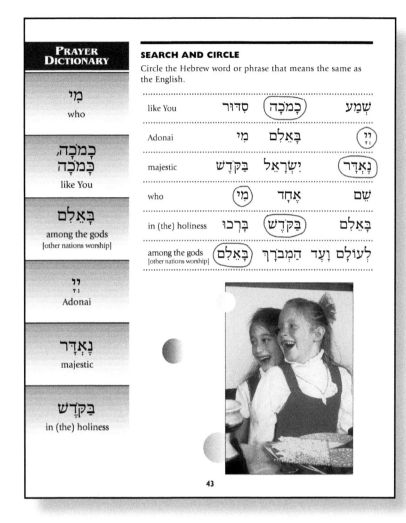

Photo Op

What are the girls eating? (*matzah*)

What is the connection between matzah and the prayer מִי כָמֹכָה? (*matzah is the symbol of the bread that did not have time to rise as we hurried to freedom; when we crossed the sea, we sang* מִי כָמֹכָה *in praise of God*)

Extending the Opportunity

Bring matzah to class. Call on each student to read or sing the prayer on page 42 with expressions of excitement and gratitude. After a student reads or sings the prayer, give him or her a piece of matzah to continue the celebration.

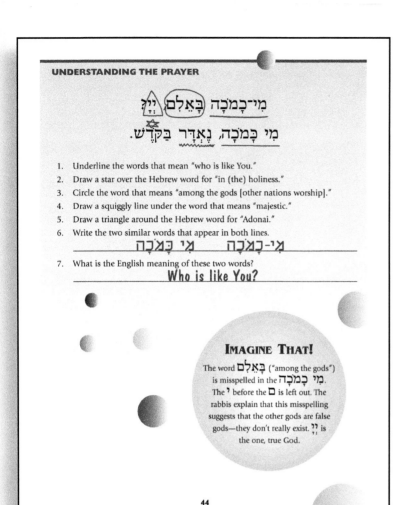

UNDERSTANDING THE PRAYER

מִי־כָמֹכָה בָּאֵלִם יְיָ

מִי כָּמֹכָה, נֶאְדָּר בַּקֹּדֶשׁ.

1. Underline the words that mean "who is like You."
2. Draw a star over the Hebrew word for "in (the) holiness."
3. Circle the word that means "among the gods [other nations worship]."
4. Draw a squiggly line under the word that means "majestic."
5. Draw a triangle around the Hebrew word for "Adonai."
6. Write the two similar words that appear in both lines.

מִי־כָמֹכָה   מִי כָּמֹכָה

7. What is the English meaning of these two words?

Who is like You?

IMAGINE THAT!

The word בָּאֵלִם ("among the gods") is misspelled in the מִי כָמֹכָה. The י before the ל is left out. The rabbis explain that this misspelling suggests that the other gods are false gods—they don't really exist. יְיָ is the one, true God.

44

UNDERSTANDING THE PRAYER

Use this exercise to reinforce the vocabulary of the prayer. Direct the students to complete it individually. Review their responses. Note: In Hebrew there is no equivalent for the English word "is." Therefore, the answer for #7, "who like You," should be "who *is* like You" to form a correct English sentence. Check that students write the word *You* with a capital "Y."

IMAGINE THAT!

Ask the students who the other gods might have been. *(idols; gods of nature)* Ask your class what other false gods people worship today. *(wealth; power; fame; ego)*

THE HOLIDAY CONNECTION

Discuss and complete "The Holiday Connection" with the class.

AN ETHICAL ECHO

Design a bulletin board which highlights the mitzvah פִּדְיוֹן שְׁבוּיִים—redeeming captives. Put the title "Captivity" or "Slavery" at the top of one side, and the title "Freedom" or "Independence" at the top of the other side. Discuss the many forms of captivity. (*famine, war, poverty, suppression*) Assign students to look through newspapers and magazines for articles about those still in captivity and for articles about former captives who are now free, and to bring the articles to class. Discuss the issues. Display the articles on the appropriate side of the bulletin board.

THE HOLIDAY CONNECTION

Legend has it that in order to gather the Jews to fight their enemy King Antiochus in ancient days, the Jewish leader, Judah, called out the first words of the מִי כָמֹכָה. The first letters of these words then became the freedom fighters' name—the Maccabees. We celebrate the victory of the Maccabees in winning religious freedom on Ḥanukkah. And some people believe that the story of Ḥanukkah—where one little pitcher of olive oil provided enough oil for the menorah to be lighted for eight long days— is another miracle!

Write the first letter of each Hebrew word in the spaces below.

מִי כָמְכָה בָּאֵלִם יְיָ

י ב כ מ

What does this word spell? _____ Maccabee

Why do you think Judah chose this prayer to rally the Jews together?
shows faith in God; acknowledges God's awesome power; recalls the miracle of the Sea of Reeds

An Ethical Echo

Throughout the ages the Jewish people have experienced captivity and freedom, slavery and independence. We know how precious freedom is. And we are determined to rescue those who are not free.

We call this the mitzvah of *Pidyon Shevuyim*—
פִּדְיוֹן שְׁבוּיִים—Redeeming Captives.

Think About This!

In what ways do we try to bring freedom to other people in the world?

45

THINK ABOUT THIS!

Discuss with your students specific steps that they could take to help free others from different forms of captivity. (*poverty: food drives, clothing drives, holiday gift drives; political suppression: letter writing, participating in forums addressing oppressed people; disease: tzedakah donations to organizations that work to find cures or help those who are ill*)

IN THE SYNAGOGUE

Read and complete page 46 with your students.

Teach students to sing מִי כָמֹכָה with the melody used in your synagogue services.

Siddur Search

מִי כָמֹכָה is recited after the שְׁמַע and the וְאָהַבְתָּ. It comes toward the ending of the blessing for redemption, *Birkat Ge'ulah*. The first three lines and the last line (יְיָ יִמְלֹךְ לְעוֹלָם וָעֶד), which are the same in the morning and evening services, come directly from the Torah (Exodus 15:11, 18).

Ask students to find the מִי כָמֹכָה in the siddur in both the evening and morning services. Ask them to look at the portion of the prayer found between the first three lines and the last line, and to note the differences in that portion between the evening and morning service.

Add the word יִמְלֹךְ to the fruit tree for the root מ ל כ.

The reproduced student page 46:

IN THE SYNAGOGUE

The prayer מִי כָמֹכָה is from the Torah. It appears in the Book of Exodus. Exodus tells the story of our people's journey from slavery in Egypt to freedom. מִי כָמֹכָה appears in the Torah after the Children of Israel have safely crossed the Sea of Reeds.

Today, מִי כָמֹכָה is read at both the morning and evening services in the synagogue.

Practice reading מִי כָמֹכָה.

1. מִי־כָמֹכָה בָּאֵלִם, יְיָ? — *Who is like You among the gods [other nations worship], Adonai?*
2. מִי כָמֹכָה, נֶאְדָּר בַּקֹּדֶשׁ, — *Who is like You, majestic in (the) holiness,*
3. נוֹרָא תְהִלֹּת, עֹשֵׂה פֶלֶא? — *Awesome in splendor, doing wonders?*

Now read the line following מִי כָמֹכָה.

יְיָ יִמְלֹךְ לְעוֹלָם וָעֶד.
Adonai will rule forever and ever.

Which three letters in יִמְלֹךְ tell us that "rule" is part of the word's meaning?

Write the three letters. כ ל מ

These three letters are called the ___root___.

Write the phrase that means "forever and ever." לְעוֹלָם וָעֶד

46

TRUE OR FALSE

Direct students to complete this section independently. When reviewing students' answers, call upon them to correct the statements that did not receive a check mark. Ask them to change the one word in each sentence to a word that would make the sentence true. *(sentence 2: twice a day; sentence 4: Book of Exodus)*

ROOTS

Write the word שֹׁרֶשׁ on the chalkboard. Ask the students to read this double-dot word correctly. Tell them the word means "root." Write the שֹׁרֶשׁ—the root—ק ד שׁ on the board. Then write its English meaning ("holy," "unlike any other"). Write examples such as the following for students to read: קָדוֹשׁ קָדוֹשׁ קֹדֶשׁ.

When a word begins קָ, the vowel ָ usually makes the same special sound as in the words כָּל and כָּל (*oh* or *aw*).

Practice reading: קָדְשׁוּ קָדְשֶׁךָ קָדְשׁוֹ.

Then, read and complete "Roots" with the students.

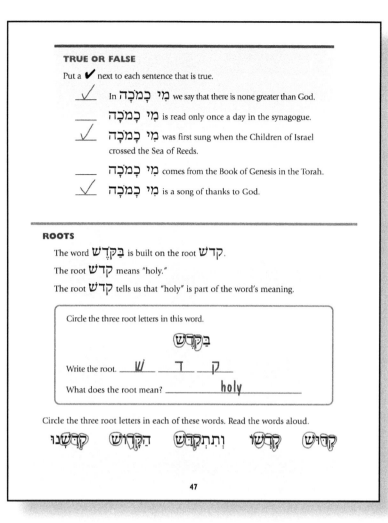

The Fruit of the Tree

Create a new tree with three roots from oaktag. Write the letters ק ד שׁ on the three roots—one letter on each root. Write the meaning, "holy," on the trunk of the tree. Create fruit for the tree (a fruit you have not yet used)—one for each of the words: קָדוֹשׁ קָדִישׁ קָדוֹשׁ קָדֻשָׁה. Discuss the significance of these words. Then, add in any additional words from the "Roots" exercise which are not already on the tree.

BACK TO THE SOURCES

This is a page from the Book of Exodus. It is the song the Children of Israel sang after they crossed the Sea of Reeds. The Torah says that the waters of the Sea of Reeds formed a wall to the right and to the left of the Children of Israel as they crossed on dry land. Do you think the text resembles a wall of bricks?

Can you find and read the first three lines of מִי כָמֹכָה?

Can you find and read the line following מִי כָמֹכָה?

48

BACK TO THE SOURCES

Explain that this is a page from the *Ḥumash*. It resembles the passage as it appears in the Torah. However, in the *Sefer Torah*—the Torah Scroll—there are only Hebrew letters, while in the *Ḥumash* there are also vowels, *trope* marks, and verses indicated by numerals (1, 2, 3 . . .) or by Hebrew letters which represent numbers. (See verse 10, which is noted with the letter י and verse 15 which is noted with the letters טו.) Sometimes a verse begins in the middle of a line. (See verse 11—מִי־כָמֹכָה.) Sometimes two verses begin in the middle of a line. (See verses 12—נָטִיתָ and 13—נָחִיתָ.)

Direct students' attention to the *trope* marks. They indicate the melody for chanting the words of Torah.

Read the introduction on page 48 with your students. Have students find and read the verses in answer to the two questions. (See verses 11 and 18.)

In the Synagogue

Take the students to the sanctuary, and open the *Sefer Torah* to the song we sang at the Sea of Reeds. Ask students the same two questions found on the top of page 48. If possible, invite a Torah reader from your congregation to chant the first and last lines of מִי כָמֹכָה in Torah *trope*. Call on the class to chant together from the Torah. Students can take turns being the Torah reader and using the *yad* to point to the words.

PRAYER BUILDING BLOCKS

Read and complete this section together with students.

READING PRACTICE

Call on students to read:

- the two words built on the root ק ד שׁ

  (בְּקֹדֶשׁ   בִּקְדֻשָׁתוֹ)

- the six words with a silent *dagesh*

  (בַּקֹדֶשׁ בִּקְדֻשָׁתוֹ בַּשָׁמַיִם בַּיוֹם בַּיָמִים בַּזְמַן)

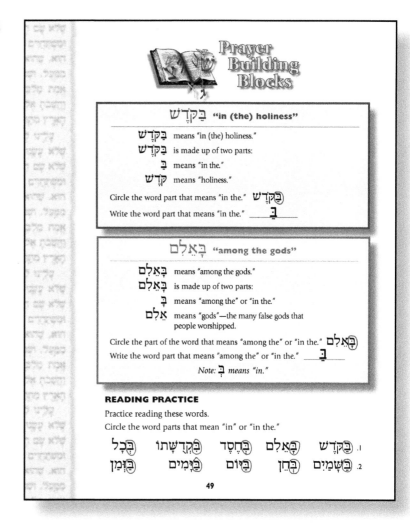

FLUENT READING

Practice reading the lines below.

מִי־כָמְכָה בָּאֵלִם, יְיָ? .1

מִי כָּמְכָה, נֶאְדָּר בַּקֹּדֶשׁ, .2

נוֹרָא תְהִלֹּת, עֹשֵׂה פֶלֶא? .3

מִי כָמוֹךָ, בַּעַל גְּבוּרוֹת, וּמִי דוֹמֶה לָךְ? .4

אֵין כָּמוֹךָ חַנּוּן וְרַחוּם, יְיָ אֱלֹהֵינוּ. .5

אֵין כָּמוֹךָ, אֵל, אֶרֶךְ אַפַּיִם וְרַב חֶסֶד וֶאֱמֶת. .6

רַחֵם עָלֵינוּ וְעַל כָּל מַעֲשֶׂיךָ, כִּי אֵין כָּמוֹךָ, יְיָ אֱלֹהֵינוּ. .7

תְּהִלַּת יְיָ יְדַבֶּר פִּי, וִיבָרֵךְ כָּל בָּשָׂר שֵׁם קָדְשׁוֹ. .8

מִי יַעֲלֶה בְהַר יְיָ, וּמִי יָקוּם בִּמְקוֹם קָדְשׁוֹ? .9

וְאַתָּה קָדוֹשׁ, יוֹשֵׁב תְּהִלּוֹת יִשְׂרָאֵל. .10

50

WORKSHEET

Use the worksheet for Lesson 5 to review vocabulary and the concepts underlying the prayer.

FAMILY EDUCATION

Duplicate and send home with students the Family Education page, "As a Family: Crossing the Sea" (at the back of this guide).

Encourage students to share their families' responses with the class.

FLUENT READING

Reading Skills

Call on students individually to find and read a word from the categories listed below. After the student finds and reads a word, call on another student to read the complete phrase (comma to comma) that contains the word.

- words built on the root ק ד שׁ (lines 2 and 8–10)
- the word built on the root ב ר כ (line 8)
- phrases with some form or variation of the word כָּמֹכָה (lines 1, 2, and 4–7)

Vocabulary Recognition

Give students the clues below, and ask them to find and read the correct word or phrase based on the clue. To focus their attention on a limited number of lines but avoid making it *too* easy, ask them to choose from the lines listed below—the underlined number indicates the correct line where the word or phrase can be found. To make the activity more difficult, don't limit their choice of lines.

- the phrase with the word meaning "our God" (אֱלֹהֵינוּ —line 1 or 5 or 8)
- the Hebrew word meaning "Israel" (line 6 or 8 or 10 —יִשְׂרָאֵל)
- the phrase for God's "holy name" (line 2 or 8 or 10—שֵׁם קָדְשׁוֹ)
- the phrase meaning "Who is like You" (line 1 or 2 or 9—מִי כָּמֹכָה and מִי כָמוֹךָ)

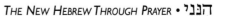

HOME RITUALS AND BLESSINGS

Read the first paragraph together with students.

To provide a break point as you move into the second half of the textbook, design a "Student Service" by assigning a leadership role for each of Lessons 1–5 to five different students, and then ask the congregation of students to read or sing the prayers in these lessons.

Read the second paragraph together with students. Ask them to share rituals they have experienced in their homes or in the homes of relatives and friends.

HOME RITUALS AND BLESSINGS

The prayers you have learned so far in this book can be heard in synagogue when we gather as a community to celebrate Shabbat or the holidays. They are a part of our synagogue services. For example, do you remember that the בָּרְכוּ is the prayer that calls the congregation together to start the service? And that the שְׁמַע is the prayer the congregation says to declare our belief in only one God?

There are blessings we say, too. We say them at home, as part of the rituals and ceremonies we celebrate with our moms and dads, brothers and sisters, cousins, grandmothers and grandfathers. We light Ḥanukkah candles and we sit and eat in a sukkah; we say Kiddush on a Friday night and we say thank you to God with a blessing after we have eaten. You will learn about all these blessings and rituals in the next section.

Name: _____

מִי כָמֹכָה

1. When did the Jews first sing מִי כָמֹכָה? _____

   _____

2. Why did they sing this song?

   _____

3. Which book of the Torah contains this song? _____

4. Number the three lines to place the מִי כָמֹכָה prayer in the correct order.

   Then number the English to match the Hebrew.

   _____ Who is like You, majestic in holiness   נוֹרָא תְהִלֹת, עֹשֵׂה פֶּלֶא _____

   _____ Who is like You among the gods,
   (other nations worship), Adonai   מִי כָמֹכָה, נֶאְדָּר בַּקֹּדֶשׁ _____

   _____ Awesome in splendor, doing wonders   מִי-כָמֹכָה בָּאֵלִם, יְיָ _____

5. According to a legend, how did the Maccabees get their name?

   _____

   _____

6. Draw a line to match each root with its meaning.

   rule   ק ד שׁ

   holy   א ה ב

   bless, praise   מ ל כ

   love   ב ר כ

7. Write the correct root below each word.

   מַלְכוּתוֹ   הַמְבֹרָךְ   וְאָהַבְתָּ   יִמְלֹךְ   בָּרְכוּ   קַדֵּשׁ

   _____   _____   _____   _____   _____   _____

LESSON 6 בְּרָכוֹת

LEARNING OBJECTIVES

Prayer Reading Skills

The first six words that begin a blessing:

בָּרוּךְ אַתָּה יְיָ אֱלֹהֵינוּ מֶלֶךְ הָעוֹלָם

The four additional words that make a blessing of mitzvah:

אֲשֶׁר קִדְּשָׁנוּ בְּמִצְוֹתָיו וְצִוָּנוּ

The Hebrew word בָּרוּךְ—related to בֶּרֶךְ ("knee")

The Hebrew word אַתָּה ("You," used to address God)

Suffix: יו ("his," "God's")

Roots: א מ נ ("faith"); צ ו ה ("command")

Review:

roots ב ר כ, מ ל כ, ק ד שׁ

prefix הַ, הָ ("the")

word ending נוּ ("us," "our")

vav with "o" vowel (וֹ)

Prayer Concepts

Term: אָמֵן ("Amen") said after a blessing to indicate agreement with the blessing or faith in God

BEYOND THE TEXTBOOK

Four categories of בְּרָכוֹת

Vav with *dagesh* (וּ)

SET INDUCTION

A בְּרָכָה is a blessing that praises and thanks God, Ruler of the world, for specific spiritual and material gifts. Reciting a בְּרָכָה shows our appreciation for the world around us. The בְּרָכוֹת—blessings—express a direct relationship between the worshiper and God— God is both our partner and our Ruler.

FOUR TYPES OF בְּרָכוֹת

There are four basic categories of בְּרָכוֹת:

1. Those included in regular worship services.

2. Those expressing gratitude for routine activities such as eating and drinking.

3. Those that acknowledge God as the source of all unusual, awesome, tragic, and joyous events in life such as hearing thunder or seeing a rainbow or celebrating a personal milestone.

4. Those reminding us that we are fulfilling God's מִצְוֹת —commandments. These are בְּרָכוֹת שֶׁל מִצְוָה— "blessings of mitzvah"—which lead us to actions that help us fulfill the commandment to be a holy people.

INSTRUCTIONAL MATERIALS

Text pages 52–65

Word Cards 2, 4, 19, and 35–41

Worksheet for Lesson 6

Family Education: "As a Family: Sharing Blessings" (at the back of this guide)

SET INDUCTION

Visualizing the Concept

Draw a circle on the chalkboard. Divide the circle into six pie-shaped sections. Along the perimeter label the sections as follows: family, friendships, nature, self, Judaism, Israel.

Discuss the significance of the term "appreciate." *(recognize the value of something; hold it in high esteem)* Discuss each section in the circle by challenging students to think about ways they show appreciation for each of these aspects of their lives *(e.g., how they show appreciation for the love of family; the qualities of friendship; the beauty of and bounty from nature; their own positive attributes; our Jewish heritage, Torah, and traditions; the role Israel has played and continues to play in the lives of the Jewish people)*

Ask the students: How do you show appreciation both through word and deed? How do you say "thank you"? How do you see God in each of these aspects of your life? Have students assign their blessing to the appropriate section.

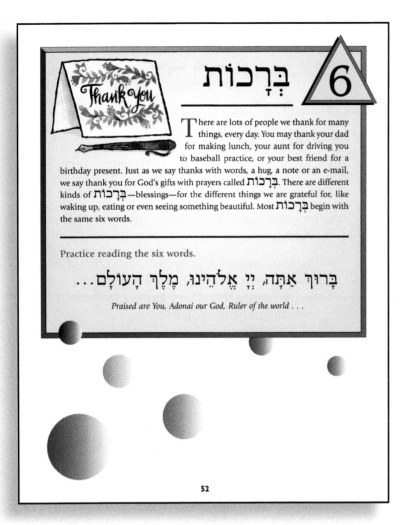

בְּרָכוֹת 6

There are lots of people we thank for many things, every day. You may thank your dad for making lunch, your aunt for driving you to baseball practice, or your best friend for a birthday present. Just as we say thanks with words, a hug, a note or an e-mail, we say thank you for God's gifts with prayers called בְּרָכוֹת. There are different kinds of בְּרָכוֹת—blessings—for the different things we are grateful for, like waking up, eating or even seeing something beautiful. Most בְּרָכוֹת begin with the same six words.

Practice reading the six words.

בָּרוּךְ אַתָּה, יְיָ אֱלֹהֵינוּ, מֶלֶךְ הָעוֹלָם...

Praised are You, Adonai our God, Ruler of the world . . .

52

INTO THE TEXT

Explain to the students that a blessing—a בְּרָכָה—is a prayer that implies "thank you."

Call on individual students to read the introduction on page 52. Then, ask the class to read aloud the first six Hebrew words that introduce Hebrew blessings. Ask them to read the English meaning. Note: Sometimes the word הָעוֹלָם is translated as "the universe."

Call on individual students:

- to recite the first six Hebrew words of a blessing

- to complete the sentence and express their appreciation by selecting from the categories previously discussed (*e.g., family: for the love of my family; nature: for food that grows from the earth; Judaism: for living where I can freely be Jewish*)

Display Word Cards 2, 4, 19, and 35–37 in random order. Call on students to place them in the correct right-to-left order.

(בָּרוּךְ אַתָּה יְיָ אֱלֹהֵינוּ מֶלֶךְ הָעוֹלָם)

For Discussion

Why do you think we use the same six words to begin every blessing? (*the repetition eases us into blessings; they provide a familiar framework within which we can express our appreciation; they reinforce the idea that no matter what we are thankful for, the source of it is the same—God*)

PRAYER DICTIONARY

Word Cards

Display Hebrew Word Cards 2, 4, 19, and 35–37. Have students turn over their books. Call on a student to come to the front of the class and "be the teacher." That student calls out the Hebrew word on a Word Card and the other students respond with the English translation. The "teacher" confirms the answer by showing the back of the Word Card with the English translation. Then, change the activity by calling on another student to be "teacher," and this time to call out the English word first.

SEARCH AND CIRCLE

Direct students to complete the exercise individually. Have them cover the Prayer Dictionary while completing the exercise and then have them uncover it to self-check their answers.

FIND THE WORDS

Allow students several minutes to complete the exercise and then share their answers.

Tic-Tac-Toe Challenge

Draw a new Tic-Tac-Toe grid on the chalkboard. In the nine squares write the English meanings of nine words not circled in the "Search and Circle" exercise. Divide the class into two teams. Ask the players on each team to read the English words and give the corresponding Hebrew meaning for each. In this way, students will review previously learned prayer vocabulary. *(meanings of words not circled from right to left: line 1—You, name; line 2— Israel, glory of; line 3—like You, majestic; line 4— God's kingdom, among the gods (other nations worship); line 5—in (the) holiness, hear; line 6—one, who)*

BEGINNINGS AND ENDINGS

For each blessing, underline the six words that usually begin a בְּרָכָה—a blessing.

1. בָּרוּךְ אַתָּה, יְיָ אֱלֹהֵינוּ, מֶלֶךְ הָעוֹלָם, (בּוֹרֵא פְּרִי הַגָּפֶן.)

2. בָּרוּךְ אַתָּה, יְיָ אֱלֹהֵינוּ, מֶלֶךְ הָעוֹלָם, (הַמּוֹצִיא לֶחֶם מִן הָאָרֶץ.)

3. בָּרוּךְ אַתָּה, יְיָ אֱלֹהֵינוּ, מֶלֶךְ הָעוֹלָם, (בּוֹרֵא מִינֵי מְזוֹנוֹת.)

Now *write* the words that usually begin a בְּרָכָה.

בָּרוּךְ אַתָּה, יְיָ אֱלֹהֵינוּ, מֶלֶךְ הָעוֹלָם

*The first six words of a blessing are usually the same,
but the ending changes according to what you are thanking God for.*

Circle the endings of the three blessings above.

Which of these blessings is said over ḥallah? Write the number: __2__

DID YOU KNOW?

When we finish saying a blessing, the people around us respond with "Amen."

What does "Amen" mean?

Amen comes from the root אמן which means "believe" or "have faith." (אֱמוּנָה, "faith," comes from the same root.) When we say Amen, we are showing that we agree with the person who is saying the blessing. We are expressing our faith in God.

54

BEGINNINGS AND ENDINGS

Complete the "Beginnings" component of the exercise together. Call on students to read aloud the beginnings they have underlined.

Then complete the "Endings" component of the exercise together. Call on students to read aloud the endings they have circled.

DID YOU KNOW?

Read the explanation with students.

Call on individual students to read the three blessings at the top of page 54. At the conclusion of each blessing, ask the class to respond by saying "Amen."

The Fruit of the Tree

Create a new fruit tree with three roots. Write the letters א מ נ on the three roots—one letter on each root. Then write its meaning ("faith") on the trunk of the tree. Create a new kind of fruit for the tree, and make fruit for the words אָמֵן and אֱמוּנָה.

PRAYER BUILDING BLOCKS

בָּרוּך "blessed" or "praised"

Read the explanation aloud with students. Explain that the Jewish people do not usually kneel when praying. However, it was once the custom, when addressing the ruler of a country, to kneel before the ruler.

Add the word בֶּרֶךְ to the fruit of the tree ב ר כ.

For Discussion

At times while reciting a blessing that is part of the prayer service, we bend our knees and bow when saying the word בָּרוּך. What do you think this action symbolizes? (*respect for God; appreciation; humility*)

אַתָּה "you"

Read the explanation aloud with students. Have them fill in the missing English and Hebrew words. Call on one student to be the reader. Ask the Reader to read the introductory words of a blessing to the class, but to pause before saying אַתָּה. Ask the class to read אַתָּה in unison when the Reader gets there. Then have the Reader complete the passage.

For Discussion

Have students describe a relationship they have with a close friend, and ask them:

- What makes the person a close friend?

- What expectations do you have in such a relationship?

- Can your friend always do what you want?

- What happens in the relationship when things don't go the way you want?

Photo Op

- How do we know the girls are enjoying themselves? (*they are smiling*) What are they enjoying? (*the sweetness of their food; their friendship*)

- What blessing would they say before eating ḥallah or other bread to show they are grateful for this food? (הַמּוֹצִיא) Recite הַמּוֹצִיא together as a class (page 54, line 2).

- How does our partnership with God enable the girls to have the ḥallah to enjoy? (*God provides the world in which grain can grow; people harvest the grain, treat the grain, create dough, etc.*)

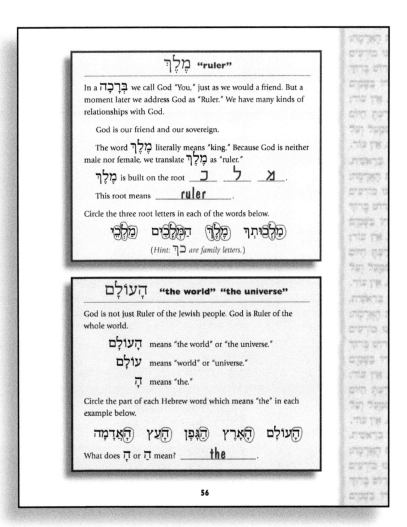

מֶלֶךְ "ruler"

In a בְּרָכָה we call God "You," just as we would a friend. But a moment later we address God as "Ruler." We have many kinds of relationships with God.

God is our friend and our sovereign.

The word מֶלֶךְ literally means "king." Because God is neither male nor female, we translate מֶלֶךְ as "ruler."

מֶלֶךְ is built on the root מ ל כ.

This root means **ruler**.

Circle the three root letters in each of the words below.

מַלְכוּתְךָ   מֶלֶךְ   הַמְּלָכִים   מַלְכִּי

(*Hint:* כ ך *are family letters.*)

הָעוֹלָם "the world" "the universe"

God is not just Ruler of the Jewish people. God is Ruler of the whole world.

הָעוֹלָם means "the world" or "the universe."

עוֹלָם means "world" or "universe."

הָ means "the."

Circle the part of each Hebrew word which means "the" in each example below.

הָעוֹלָם   הָאָרֶץ   הַגָּפֶן   הָעֵץ   הָאֲדָמָה

What does הָ or הַ mean? **the**

56

PRAYER BUILDING BLOCKS

מֶלֶךְ "ruler"

Draw two columns on the chalkboard. Label one "Friend" and one "Ruler." Ask students for words and phrases that describe the qualities of each. (*Ruler: sets laws; governs; keeps a people together; Friend: listens; understands; shows compassion; offers support*) Discuss people who are in a position of authority and yet are still friends. (*teacher, rabbi, sports coach, music instructor*)

Read the introductory paragraph on page 56 with the students. Look once again at the words and phrases under the two categories on the chalkboard. How do these terms describe God's roles in their lives?

Ask the class to fill in the blanks on the top half of the page.

Add the words at the bottom of the first building block to the fruit of the tree מ ל כ.

הָעוֹלָם "the world," "the universe"

Read this section with the students. Ask them to recite the first six words of a blessing—the phrase that ends with the word הָעוֹלָם. (This is the first word in the list at the bottom of page 56.) Ask students if they know the four blessings that conclude with the remaining four words at the bottom of the page. Ask them when we recite each of those blessings.

before a meal containing bread	הַמּוֹצִיא לֶחֶם מִן הָאָרֶץ
before drinking wine or grape juice	בּוֹרֵא פְּרִי הַגָּפֶן
before eating fruit that grows on a tree	בּוֹרֵא פְּרִי הָעֵץ
before eating food that grows in the ground	בּוֹרֵא פְּרִי הָאֲדָמָה

BIRKAT HAMAZON

Read the introduction with students. Ask them to find and lightly circle the word מָזוֹן ("food") in the prayer (lines 6 and 8) and the word meaning "bread" (לֶחֶם, line 4). If they need a hint, tell them to think of the blessing over bread before a meal—they can look at the blessing on page 57.

Reading Skills

There are many words in בִּרְכַּת הַמָּזוֹן with the "oo" and "o" vowel sounds. For fun, have the class form two groups by counting off "oo," "o," "oo," "o" (instead of 1-2, 1-2). Ask each group to highlight or circle all the words with their assigned vowel sound, and then to meet and practice saying those words. Convene the groups. Call on individual students to read a word, alternating between groups, or ask one student from each group to read all of the group's words.

Number Games
Number Line

Write the numbers 1–9 on individual slips of paper and place them in a box. Pass the box around the room and have nine students select a slip of paper. Call on these students to stand in right-to-left line order (9–1) and read the corresponding line in the passage on page 59. Put the numbers back in the box and play again, allowing those students who did not play in the first round a turn.

Tic-Tac-Toe

Divide the class into two teams and draw a Tic-Tac-Toe grid on the chalkboard. Write numbers 1–9 in random order in the squares. Each team, alternating, selects a box in the grid and reads the line from page 59 indicated by the number in the box. If the player reads the line correctly, the team mark is placed in the box. If not, the other team gets a chance.

בִּרְכַּת הַמָּזוֹן

How do you feel after you've finished a delicious dinner that your mom or dad made? Probably full and happy—and pleased that they took the time to cook for you. Just as you thank your mom or dad after dinner for preparing such a great meal, we thank God after our meal by saying בִּרְכַּת הַמָּזוֹן.

בִּרְכַּת הַמָּזוֹן thanks God for more than providing us with the food we've just eaten. It also thanks God for the Land of Israel and the Torah, and it praises God's goodness and kindness. We enjoy feeling full—filled with food and filled with God's gifts—and we thank God for allowing us to enjoy them all.

Practice reading this section of בִּרְכַּת הַמָּזוֹן.

1. בָּרוּךְ אַתָּה, יְיָ אֱלֹהֵינוּ, מֶלֶךְ הָעוֹלָם,
2. הַזָּן אֶת הָעוֹלָם כֻּלּוֹ בְּטוּבוֹ,
3. בְּחֵן בְּחֶסֶד וּבְרַחֲמִים.
4. הוּא נוֹתֵן לֶחֶם לְכָל בָּשָׂר, כִּי לְעוֹלָם חַסְדּוֹ.
5. וּבְטוּבוֹ הַגָּדוֹל תָּמִיד לֹא חָסַר לָנוּ,
6. וְאַל יֶחְסַר לָנוּ מָזוֹן לְעוֹלָם וָעֶד.
7. בַּעֲבוּר שְׁמוֹ הַגָּדוֹל כִּי הוּא אֵל זָן וּמְפַרְנֵס לַכֹּל,
8. וּמֵטִיב לַכֹּל, וּמֵכִין מָזוֹן לְכָל בְּרִיּוֹתָיו אֲשֶׁר בָּרָא.
9. בָּרוּךְ אַתָּה יְיָ, הַזָּן אֶת הַכֹּל.

DID YOU KNOW?
The full בִּרְכַּת הַמָּזוֹן is said only after a meal at which bread has been consumed. You can see how important bread really is.

59

Reading and Singing

Read the blessing together with students. Teach students the melody and sing it together.

Extending the Lesson

Ask your students to write to the organization, Mazon: The Jewish Response to Hunger. Instruct your students: Learn about their work. How can you help the organization? How can you help the hungry in your community?

בִּרְכוֹת שֶׁל מִצְוָה

We also say a בְּרָכָה when we carry out certain commandments from God. All of God's commandments are known as mitzvot, and particular ones—like studying Torah, blowing the shofar on the High Holy Days, or sitting and eating in a sukkah on Sukkot—require us to say a blessing when we perform them. Every בְּרָכָה שֶׁל מִצְוָה begins with the same ten words.

Practice reading these words.

1. בָּרוּךְ אַתָּה, יְיָ אֱלֹהֵינוּ, מֶלֶךְ הָעוֹלָם,

2. אֲשֶׁר קִדְּשָׁנוּ בְּמִצְוֹתָיו וְצִוָּנוּ...

Praised are You, Adonai our God, Ruler of the world,
who makes us holy with God's commandments and commands us . . .

Think About This!

Because so many of God's commandments—mitzvot—require us to be good and decent, many people consider a mitzvah to be a "good deed." You perform mitzvot every day without even realizing it—like visiting your best friend when she's home with a cold, trying not to gossip about kids at school, or even feeding your puppy before you eat your own dinner! What other kinds of "good deed" mitzvot do you do?

60

בִּרְכוֹת שֶׁל מִצְוָה

For Discussion

What does the term "command" mean? *(order with authority)*

What is the difference between a command and a request? *(the first you must do; the second is your choice)*

Why are commands important? *(in many cases, someone has to be in charge to make sure certain things happen; this can be a parent, teacher, coach, or other leader)*

INTO THE TEXT

Call on students to read the introduction on page 60. Have them read lines 1 and 2 in Hebrew and in English. Have them read in unison and individually.

Display Word Cards 38–41 (אֲשֶׁר קִדְּשָׁנוּ בְּמִצְוֹתָיו וְצִוָּנוּ) in random order. Call on students to place them in the correct right-to-left order. Then have them read in unison.

Display Word Cards 2, 4, 19, and 35–41 in random order. Call on students individually to place them in the correct right-to-left order. Have them read in unison. Repeat the activity.

PRAYER DICTIONARY

Word Cards

Display Word Cards 38–41. Ask students individually to:

- Read each one in turn.

- Identify the word that means "makes us holy." Clue: Look for the root that means "holy." (ק ד ש).

- Identify the word that means "and commands us." (וְצִוָּנוּ) Look for the word ending that means "us." (נוּ)

- Identify the word that means "with God's commandments." (בְּמִצְוֹתָיו)

- Identify the word that means "who." (אֲשֶׁר)

WORD MATCH

Direct students to complete the exercise individually. Ask them to cover the Prayer Dictionary while working on the exercise. When finished, they can uncover the Prayer Dictionary to self-check.

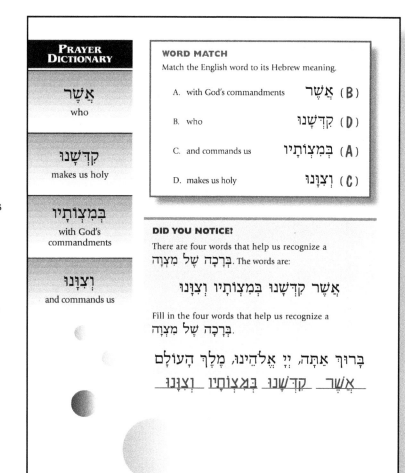

PRAYER BUILDING BLOCKS

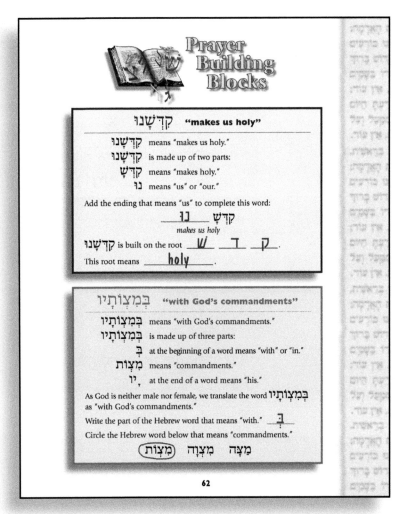

קִדְּשָׁנוּ "makes us holy"

Direct students to complete the section individually. Read it aloud together.

For Discussion

The Torah says:

קְדֹשִׁים תִּהְיוּ כִּי קָדוֹשׁ אֲנִי יְיָ אֱלֹהֵיכֶם.

"You shall be holy for I, Adonai your God, am holy." (Leviticus 19:2)

Write the verse in Hebrew and English on the chalkboard. Call on students to read the verse and locate the two words built on the root קדש. (קָדֹשִׁים קָדוֹשׁ)

Ask the students:

- Why are we a holy people? (*God commanded us to be holy*)

- What does it mean to be a holy people? (*act in the spirit of having been created in God's image; live by God's commandments; teach God's commandments and our tradition to future generations*)

You may wish to review the "Ethical Echo" discussions in the textbook on pages 26, 30, 38, 45, and 58 to assist students in responding to the last question.

Add קִדְּשָׁנוּ, קָדוֹשׁ, and קְדֹשִׁים to the fruit tree for the root ק ד שׁ.

בְּמִצְוֹתָיו "with God's commandments"

Remind students that they previously learned that the prefix בַּ or בְּ means "in the" or "among." Write בְּ, meaning "with" or "in," on the chalkboard. Read and complete page 62 with the students.

וְצִוָּנוּ "and commands us"

Reading Rule Review:

Write the letter ו on the chalkboard. Add a *dagesh*, a dot in the middle of the letter, so it looks like וּ. Now, it looks like a vowel. We know it is a letter with a *dagesh* if:

- the letter preceding it already has a vowel (צַוּ), or
- the symbol וּ has its own vowel (צִוָ).

Write the word וְצִוָּנוּ on the chalkboard. Call on a student to circle the letter *vav* and its vowel (וָ). Call on students to read the complete word.

Read and complete the page with the students.

Write the following words on the chalkboard. Ask the students to read each word. Call students individually up to the board to draw a circle around the letters in each word indicating that "command" is part of the word's meaning.

מִצְוָה וְצִוָּנוּ מִצְוֹת מְצַוֶּךְ בְּמִצְוֹתָיו

Tell students that the third root letter is ה. In many words, when ה is the third root letter, the ה falls away.

The Fruit of the Tree

Create a new fruit tree with three roots. Write the letters צ ו ה on the three roots—one letter on each root. Write the meaning, "command," on the trunk of the tree. Create a new fruit for the tree, and make pieces of fruit for each word above. Remind students that the ה has fallen away in several words.

Fruit Salad

Remove the fruit from the following fruit trees:

אהב, מלכ, ערב, ברכ,
צוה, אמנ, קדש.

Mix up the "fruit" (in a bowl if possible) to create a "fruit salad." Have students sort the fruit according to their roots and place each one on the correct tree. Have students read the word on each fruit as it "grows" back on the tree.

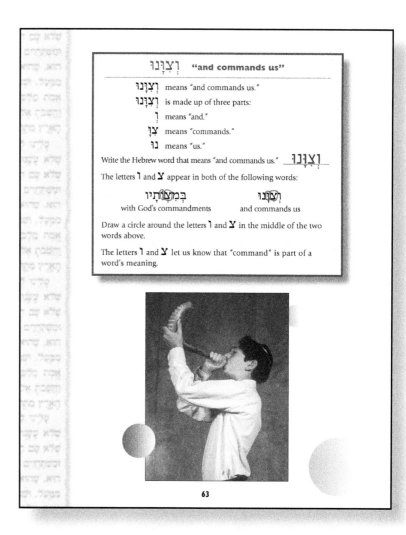

Photo Op

What is the boy doing in this photo? (*blowing shofar*) What is the holiday connection? (*Rosh Hashanah; the end of Yom Kippur*) Soon students will study the blessing for the sounding of the shofar (textbook page 78).

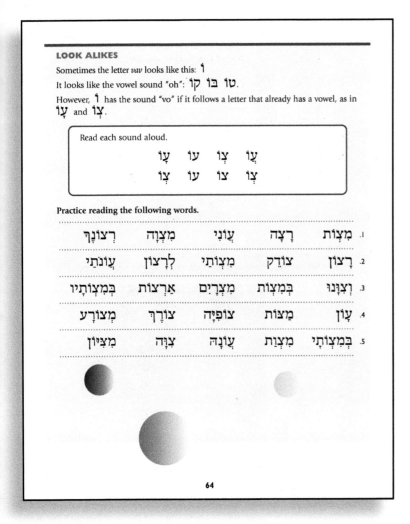

LOOK ALIKES

Sometimes the letter *vav* looks like this: וֹ

It looks like the vowel sound "oh": טוֹ בוֹ קוֹ.

However, וֹ has the sound "vo" if it follows a letter that already has a vowel, as in עָוֹ and צְוֹ.

> Read each sound aloud.
>
> עָוֹ צְוֹ עָוֹ עָוֹ
> צְוֹ עָוֹ צְוֹ צְוֹ

Practice reading the following words.

מִצְוֹת	רָצָה	עֲוֹנִי	מִצְוָה	רְצוֹנֶךָ	1
רָצוֹן	צוֹדֵק	מִצְוֹתַי	לִרְצוֹן	עֲוֹנֹתַי	2
וְצִוָּנוּ	בְּמִצְוֹת	מִצְרַיִם	אַרְצוֹת	בְּמִצְוֹתָיו	3
עָוֹן	מַצּוֹת	צוֹפִיָּה	צוֹרֶךְ	מְצוֹרָע	4
בְּמִצְוֹתַי	עֹנָה	עוֹנָה	צֻוָּה	מִצִּיוֹן	5

64

High Five

Challenge each student to give a "high five" by reading all five words on a line. Each time the student correctly reads a word, that student holds up one more finger (first the thumb, then each of the next four fingers in turn) until the student gives a "high five."

LOOK ALIKES

Explain to the class that you are going to write letter-vowel combinations on the chalkboard and all the vowels will be in color. Write the letter-vowel combinations טוֹ, בוֹ, קוֹ on the board. Use colored chalk for the vowel וֹ. Call on students to read these three combinations.

Now write the word-parts עָוֹ and צְוֹ on the board. Use colored chalk for the vowel under the ע (ָ) and the vowel under the צ (ְ) and the dot over each וֹ (ֹ). Note: Although it looks as if the first letter in each word-part (עָוֹ and צְוֹ) has two vowels, that is not possible.

Reading Rule:

The symbol וֹ says "vo" if it follows a letter that already has a vowel. Call on students to read each word-part (עָוֹ and צְוֹ).

In Color

Using white chalk, write the following words on the chalkboard:

רָצוֹן מִצְוֹת עָוֹן מַצּוֹת עֲוֹנִי מִצְוֹתָי

Call on students to change the *vowel*, either וֹ or ֹ, from white to color. At times they will change only the dot, as in מִצְוֹת. At times they will change the complete symbol וֹ as in מַצּוֹת.

Read the top half of page 64 with students. Ask them to lightly circle each word-part that says "vo." Read the circled word-parts aloud. Then read the remaining word-parts aloud.

Direct students to lines 1–5. Ask them to lightly circle each word that contains the sound "vo." Read the circled words aloud. Then read the remaining words aloud.

FLUENT READING

Write the English meaning of the words already known to your students on the chalkboard (e.g., "the world," "and commands us," "Torah"). Call on students to come to the board and write the correct Hebrew words underneath the English, using page 65 for the correct spelling.

Call on students to read the blessing that is said when:

- we are called to the Torah for an *aliyah* (#5)
- we are about to study Torah (#6)
- we wave the lulav (#2)

WORKSHEET

Duplicate Worksheet 6 to review the words of blessings.

FAMILY EDUCATION

This family activity invites the families to share some of the experiences in their lives that they view as blessings. Each family will be asked to write a personal blessing of thanks for these gifts. They may choose to write one blessing for the entire family, or individual members may each write a blessing. (See the back of this guide for the worksheet.)

FLUENT READING

Practice reading the lines below.

1. בָּרוּךְ אַתָּה, יְיָ אֱלֹהֵינוּ, מֶלֶךְ הָעוֹלָם,
אֲשֶׁר קִדְּשָׁנוּ בְּמִצְוֹתָיו וְצִוָּנוּ לְהָנִיחַ תְּפִלִּין.

2. בָּרוּךְ אַתָּה, יְיָ אֱלֹהֵינוּ, מֶלֶךְ הָעוֹלָם,
אֲשֶׁר קִדְּשָׁנוּ בְּמִצְוֹתָיו וְצִוָּנוּ עַל נְטִילַת לוּלָב.

3. בָּרוּךְ אַתָּה, יְיָ אֱלֹהֵינוּ, מֶלֶךְ הָעוֹלָם,
אֲשֶׁר קִדְּשָׁנוּ בְּמִצְוֹתָיו וְצִוָּנוּ עַל מִצְוַת תְּפִלִּין.

4. בָּרוּךְ אַתָּה, יְיָ אֱלֹהֵינוּ, מֶלֶךְ הָעוֹלָם,
אֲשֶׁר בִּדְבָרוֹ מַעֲרִיב עֲרָבִים.

5. בָּרוּךְ אַתָּה, יְיָ אֱלֹהֵינוּ, מֶלֶךְ הָעוֹלָם,
אֲשֶׁר נָתַן לָנוּ תּוֹרַת אֱמֶת.

6. בָּרוּךְ אַתָּה, יְיָ אֱלֹהֵינוּ, מֶלֶךְ הָעוֹלָם,
אֲשֶׁר קִדְּשָׁנוּ בְּמִצְוֹתָיו וְצִוָּנוּ לַעֲסֹק בְּדִבְרֵי תוֹרָה.

65

בְּרָכוֹת

1. Number the first six words of a בְּרָכָה in the correct order.

מֶלֶךְ   _____ יְיָ   _____ הָעוֹלָם _____

אֱלֹהֵינוּ   _____ בָּרוּךְ   _____ אַתָּה   _____

Number the additional four words that are recited in בְּרָכוֹת שֶׁל מִצְוָה in the correct order.

קִדְּשָׁנוּ _____   וְצִוָּנוּ _____   אֲשֶׁר _____   בְּמִצְוֹתָיו _____

2. What three Hebrew letters tell us "holy" is part of a word's meaning? _____ _____ _____

Circle these three letters in the word קִדְּשָׁנוּ.

What two Hebrew letters tell us "command" is part of a word's meaning? _____ _____

Circle these two letters in the words בְּמִצְוֹתָיו וְצִוָּנוּ.

3. Write the number of the Hebrew word next to its English meaning.

_____ Adonai   בָּרוּךְ .1

_____ ruler   אַתָּה .2

_____ you   יְיָ .3

_____ the world, the universe   אֱלֹהֵינוּ .4

_____ praised, blessed   מֶלֶךְ .5

_____ our God   הָעוֹלָם .6

_____ with (God's) commandments   אֲשֶׁר .7

_____ who   קִדְּשָׁנוּ .8

_____ and commands us   בְּמִצְוֹתָיו .9

LESSON /7\

בְּרָכוֹת שֶׁל שַׁבָּת

LEARNING OBJECTIVES

Prayer Reading Skills

The three Shabbat blessings: over candles, wine, and bread

The blessings over light

The Havdalah blessings over wine, spices, and lights

Prayer Concepts

We welcome Shabbat with a special ceremony and blessings.

We take leave of Shabbat with a special ceremony and blessings. *Havdalah* means "separation."

The two Shabbat candles remind us of the dual commandments to *remember* Shabbat and to *observe* Shabbat.

The blessing over bread represents all the food at the table.

ABOUT THE PRAYER

At the conclusion of the six days of creation, God "blessed the seventh day and called it holy" (Genesis 2:3). We sanctify Shabbat with a special ceremony on Friday night. We recite blessings over candles, over wine, and over bread. Shabbat is a day set aside for rest from our weekday activities—it is the sanctification of time. We conclude Shabbat with a special ceremony called Havdalah, which separates the holiness of Shabbat from the everyday.

INSTRUCTIONAL MATERIALS

Text pages 66–77

Word Cards 42–52

Worksheets for Lesson 7 (two)

Family Education: "As a Family: Celebrating Shabbat" (at the back of this guide)

INTRODUCING SHABBAT

The Story of Creation

Read the story of creation with the class (Genesis 1–2:4).

* What did God create each day? *(Day 1: light; Day 2: heavens; Day 3: earth and vegetation; Day 4: sun, moon, stars; Day 5: fish and birds; Day 6: land animals and people; Day 7: God rested)*

* How was the seventh day different from the first six days of creation? *(God did not work on the seventh day; God put aside the seventh day to rest; God declared the seventh day to be holy)*

* What does it mean to say the seventh day is holy (Genesis 2:3)? *(it is unlike any other day of the week; it is a day set aside to think about God and our role in the world)*

An Art Project

Decide with students on an art form to depict the six days of creation and Shabbat; you can consider a mural, diorama, collage, mobile, or any other art form.

Follow Your Star

Draw a large Jewish star on the chalkboard. The star has seven sections: the middle and six outer triangles. Number the outer sections 1–6 and the middle section 7. Write or depict Shabbat in the middle section. Call on students to identify six activities that make Shabbat different from the other six days of the week; write them in the six outer sections of the star.

בְּרָכוֹת שֶׁל שַׁבָּת /7\

Shabbat is a time of peace, a time for family. There are special בְּרָכוֹת with which we welcome Shabbat into our homes. When we say בְּרָכוֹת over the candles, wine, and ḥallah, we are thanking God for creating the Shabbat and allowing us to celebrate it.

Practice reading the בְּרָכוֹת aloud.

1. בָּרוּךְ אַתָּה, יְיָ אֱלֹהֵינוּ, מֶלֶךְ הָעוֹלָם, אֲשֶׁר קִדְּשָׁנוּ
בְּמִצְוֹתָיו וְצִוָּנוּ לְהַדְלִיק נֵר שֶׁל שַׁבָּת.

Praised are You, Adonai our God, Ruler of the world, who makes us holy with commandments and commands us to light the Sabbath light (candles).

2. בָּרוּךְ אַתָּה, יְיָ אֱלֹהֵינוּ, מֶלֶךְ הָעוֹלָם, בּוֹרֵא פְּרִי הַגָּפֶן.

Praised are You, Adonai our God, Ruler of the world, who creates the fruit of the vine.

3. בָּרוּךְ אַתָּה, יְיָ אֱלֹהֵינוּ, מֶלֶךְ הָעוֹלָם, הַמּוֹצִיא לֶחֶם
מִן הָאָרֶץ.

Praised are You, Adonai our God, Ruler of the world, who brings forth bread from the earth.

NAME THE SHABBAT OBJECT

Complete each sentence by writing the English word or drawing a picture.

Blessing #1 is said over the	Blessing #2 is said over the	Blessing #3 is said over the
candles	wine	ḥallah

66

INTO THE TEXT

Read the introduction aloud with students. Take note of the dot under the "h" in the word "ḥallah." The dot indicates the gutteral sound of the Hebrew letter ח (חַלָּה). Sometimes we indicate this sound with the letters "ch" (as in *challah*).

Practice Reading

Allow a few moments for students to read each blessing silently. Then ask:

- Which blessing is recited to fulfill a commandment? (*candlelighting*)

- What do we call such a blessing? (*a blessing of mitzvah,* בְּרָכָה שֶׁל מִצְוָה)

- Which words indicate this is a בְּרָכָה שֶׁל מִצְוָה?
  (אֲשֶׁר קִדְּשָׁנוּ בְּמִצְוֹתָיו וְצִוָּנוּ)

- What is the English meaning of this phrase? (*who makes us holy with commandments and commands us . . .*)

Read the candlelighting blessing in unison with students. Then read the English meaning.

Read the blessings recited over wine and over bread. Then read the English meaning for each one.

Complete the exercise at the bottom of the page.

LIGHTING THE CANDLES

Read the introduction with the students. Why do we usher in Shabbat with "brightness and joy"? *(possible answers: we look forward to celebrating creation and all that God has given us; it reminds us of the brightness of our world and the brightness we can bring to others)*

Visualizing the Concept

Draw a large globe of the world, and cut out paper Shabbat "flames"; give one to each student. Ask students to write responses to the question "What can each of us do to keep the brightness of Shabbat lasting all week long?" on their Shabbat flame. Paste their responses onto the globe and display them. *(possible answers: maintain peace between yourself and others; reach out to others with acts of loving-kindness)*

PRAYER DICTIONARY

Word Cards

Display Word Cards 2, 4, 19, and 35–45 in random order.

- Call on students to place them in the correct right-to-left order to form the blessing we recite over Shabbat candles.

- Designate one student to call out the English meaning for each word in random order. Call on another student to say the matching Hebrew word.

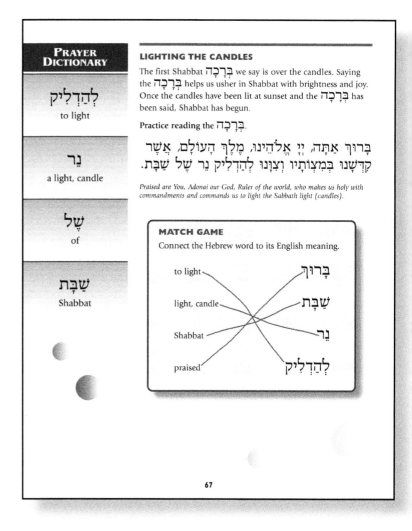

MATCH GAME

Direct students to complete the exercise individually; ask them to cover the Prayer Dictionary while completing the exercise. Then, instruct them to uncover the Prayer Dictionary to self-check. Note: Some words in the exercise were learned in previous lessons.

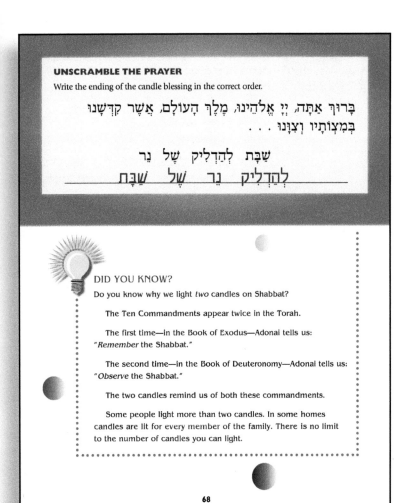

UNSCRAMBLE THE PRAYER

Display Word Cards 2, 4, 19, and 35–41 in the correct order. Place Word Cards 42–45 in scrambled order as found on the top of the page. While students unscramble the last four words in the prayer and write them on the line provided, call one student to unscramble Word Cards 42–45.

DID YOU KNOW?

Read this section aloud. Ask students: If you were to light one candle for every member of your family, how many would you light each Friday night? What might lighting candles for each family member symbolize? (*each family member is individually welcoming Shabbat; each family member feels the glow of his or her own Shabbat candle; together, the light and warmth represent family unity*)

For Discussion

- Why do you think we are instructed not only to *remember* Shabbat, but also to *observe* it? (*it is the "doing," the observing, that preserves Shabbat; the actual doing gives form and content to Shabbat*)

- In what ways do we observe Shabbat? (*through ritual: candlelighting, wine and ḥallah; by having Shabbat dinner with family and friends; by attending Shabbat services; by observing a day of rest away from the work week; traditionally, by observing the Shabbat prohibitions, e.g., not driving*)

CANDLES AND LIGHT

Read the introduction together. Direct students to read blessings 1–5 silently.

Tell your students: "These are the times we recite these blessings." Then write the following occasions on the chalkboard in random order and ask students to match each with blessings 1–5:

(a) Shabbat; (b) a holiday; (c) a holiday that begins on Shabbat; (d) Ḥanukkah; (e) Havdalah.

Direct students to blessings 1–4. Ask them:

- What phrase indicates that each is a בְּרָכָה שֶׁל מִצְוָה?
  (אֲשֶׁר קִדְּשָׁנוּ בְּמִצְוֹתָיו וְצִוָּנוּ)

- What three-word phrase follows וְצִוָּנוּ in blessings 1–4? (לְהַדְלִיק נֵר שֶׁל) What does the phrase mean? *(to light the _____ light)*

Then ask students to answer the question at the bottom of the page.

Have half the class read the ten introductory words in blessing 1. Have the other half respond with the concluding words. Repeat for blessings 2–4. Then reverse roles for each half of the class.

Direct students' attention to blessing 5, which we recite as part of the Havdalah service. Mention that they will learn this and other Havdalah blessings later on in this lesson. (See page 75 of the student text). Have the class read the blessing in unison.

CANDLES AND LIGHT

Candles and light play an important role in Judaism. The Ḥanukkah candles flicker and glow on your window ledge. We light a *yahrzeit* candle to remember the anniversary of a loved one's death. And the Eternal Light always burns above the Holy Ark.

Practice reading each of these blessings recited over candles.

1. בָּרוּךְ אַתָּה, יְיָ אֱלֹהֵינוּ, מֶלֶךְ הָעוֹלָם, אֲשֶׁר קִדְּשָׁנוּ בְּמִצְוֹתָיו וְצִוָּנוּ לְהַדְלִיק נֵר שֶׁל שַׁבָּת.

2. בָּרוּךְ אַתָּה, יְיָ אֱלֹהֵינוּ, מֶלֶךְ הָעוֹלָם, אֲשֶׁר קִדְּשָׁנוּ בְּמִצְוֹתָיו וְצִוָּנוּ לְהַדְלִיק נֵר שֶׁל יוֹם טוֹב.

3. בָּרוּךְ אַתָּה, יְיָ אֱלֹהֵינוּ, מֶלֶךְ הָעוֹלָם, אֲשֶׁר קִדְּשָׁנוּ בְּמִצְוֹתָיו וְצִוָּנוּ לְהַדְלִיק נֵר שֶׁל שַׁבָּת וְשֶׁל יוֹם טוֹב.

4. בָּרוּךְ אַתָּה, יְיָ אֱלֹהֵינוּ, מֶלֶךְ הָעוֹלָם, אֲשֶׁר קִדְּשָׁנוּ בְּמִצְוֹתָיו וְצִוָּנוּ לְהַדְלִיק נֵר שֶׁל חֲנֻכָּה.

5. בָּרוּךְ אַתָּה, יְיָ אֱלֹהֵינוּ, מֶלֶךְ הָעוֹלָם, בּוֹרֵא מְאוֹרֵי הָאֵשׁ.

Do you recognize the blessing over the Ḥanukkah candles?

Write its number here. ____4____

69

FOOD FOR THOUGHT

This is a good time for each student to practice the blessing over candles following the ritual described on this page. Bring candles and a pair of candlesticks to class. Call on each student in turn to light the candles following the candlelighting ritual. You might wish to ask students who are able to do so to bring candlesticks and candles from home.

Extending the Lesson

Invite parents to join the class for the candlelighting ritual. After each parent and child has lit the Shabbat candles, talk with them about the significance of Shabbat light. Encourage parents to share memories of their own childhood around the Shabbat table with their parents and grandparents. Encourage them to talk about family stories that reflect their Jewish experience.

Photo Op

Point out to your students that the grandmother and granddaughter have covered their eyes. Traditionally, Jewish women cover their eyes before reciting the blessing so as not to see the lit candles. They then recite the blessing, uncover their eyes, see and enjoy the light "for the first time"—*after* they have said the blessing. Direct students to read the last paragraph in "Food for Thought."

Discuss the table setting shown for Shabbat: beautiful wine goblets, tablecloth, napkins and dishes, decorative ḥallah cover, silver candlesticks. Explain: The table reflects the tradition known as הִדּוּר מִצְוָה—"beautifying the mitzvah." We honor the mitzvah by beautifying it.

Extending the Opportunity

Talk about ways we beautify the mitzvah when we celebrate other holidays such as Passover, Ḥanukkah, and Sukkot.

BLESSING FOR THE WINE

Read the introductory paragraph with students. The blessing over wine *introduces* the Kiddush. (Some people refer to the blessing over wine *as part of* the Kiddush.) The students will study the Kiddush in Lesson 9. (See textbook page 86.)

For Discussion

The wine glass overflows to thank God for the abundance of our blessings. Ask: What are the blessings in your life? *(solicit individual responses from students)*

Call on students to recite the blessing over wine.

Re-create the first two steps of the Shabbat ritual:

- Light the Shabbat candles, then recite the blessing.
- Recite the blessing over wine, then serve grape juice to your class.

Ask: Why did we first light the candles and then recite the blessing? (Refer students to the second paragraph on page 70.)

PRAYER DICTIONARY

Word Cards

Display Word Cards 46–48 in turn and ask for the meaning of each word. Place the cards in order. Ask students to translate the phrase.

Complete the exercise on page 71 and share answers.

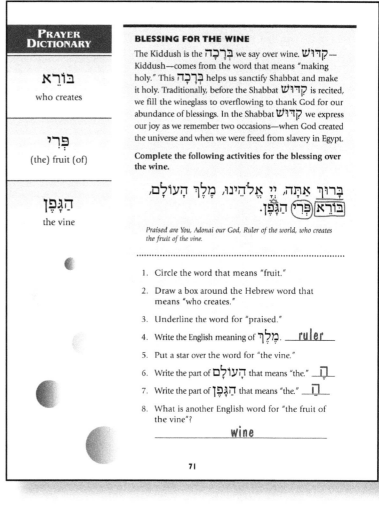

PRAYER DICTIONARY

בּוֹרֵא
who creates

פְּרִי
(the) fruit (of)

הַגָּפֶן
the vine

BLESSING FOR THE WINE

The Kiddush is the בְּרָכָה we say over wine. קִדּוּשׁ—Kiddush—comes from the word that means "making holy." This בְּרָכָה helps us sanctify Shabbat and make it holy. Traditionally, before the Shabbat קִדּוּשׁ is recited, we fill the wineglass to overflowing to thank God for our abundance of blessings. In the Shabbat קִדּוּשׁ we express our joy as we remember two occasions—when God created the universe and when we were freed from slavery in Egypt.

Complete the following activities for the blessing over the wine.

בָּרוּךְ אַתָּה, יְיָ אֱלֹהֵינוּ, מֶלֶךְ הָעוֹלָם, בּוֹרֵא פְּרִי הַגָּפֶן.

Praised are You, Adonai our God, Ruler of the world, who creates the fruit of the vine.

1. Circle the word that means "fruit."
2. Draw a box around the Hebrew word that means "who creates."
3. Underline the word for "praised."
4. Write the English meaning of מֶלֶךְ. **ruler**
5. Put a star over the word for "the vine."
6. Write the part of הָעוֹלָם that means "the." הָ
7. Write the part of הַגָּפֶן that means "the." הַ
8. What is another English word for "the fruit of the vine"? **wine**

71

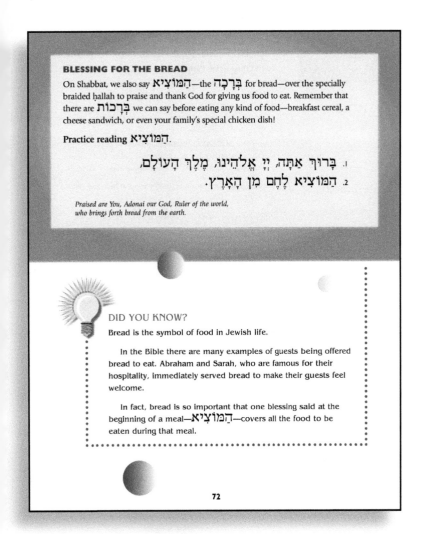

BLESSING FOR THE BREAD

On Shabbat, we also say הַמּוֹצִיא—the בְּרָכָה for bread—over the specially braided ḥallah to praise and thank God for giving us food to eat. Remember that there are בְּרָכוֹת we can say before eating any kind of food—breakfast cereal, a cheese sandwich, or even your family's special chicken dish!

Practice reading הַמּוֹצִיא.

1. בָּרוּךְ אַתָּה, יְיָ אֱלֹהֵינוּ, מֶלֶךְ הָעוֹלָם,
2. הַמּוֹצִיא לֶחֶם מִן הָאָרֶץ.

Praised are You, Adonai our God, Ruler of the world, who brings forth bread from the earth.

DID YOU KNOW?

Bread is the symbol of food in Jewish life.

In the Bible there are many examples of guests being offered bread to eat. Abraham and Sarah, who are famous for their hospitality, immediately served bread to make their guests feel welcome.

In fact, bread is so important that one blessing said at the beginning of a meal—הַמּוֹצִיא—covers all the food to be eaten during that meal.

72

DID YOU KNOW?

If there is a soup kitchen or food pantry in your community, your class might direct a schoolwide bread drive: *Leḥem for Life.* Your students can meet with other classes in the school to explain the importance of bread in Jewish life and to teach them the blessing. Ask each student to bring in a loaf of bread to be donated. (Before introducing the project, check with the soup kitchen or food pantry to be certain they can distribute the bread in a timely fashion.)

BLESSING FOR THE BREAD

If possible, bring a ḥallah to class. Read the introduction with the students. Practice the blessing over bread. Enjoy the ḥallah treat with your class.

Extending the Ritual

Traditionally, on Friday night we have two *ḥallot* (plural of ḥallah) on the Shabbat table. They symbolize the double portion of manna God provided on the sixth day of the journey of the Israelites from slavery in Egypt to freedom in Canaan (Exodus 16:22–26). In this way were we able to rest on the seventh day and not have to work at gathering food.

The cover over the ḥallah and the plate or tray under it represent the two layers of dew which protected the manna from the heat of the desert sun and the sand of the desert. The cover over the ḥallah is also said to prevent the ḥallah from being "embarrassed," since the blessing over bread is usually recited first (except on Shabbat when we highlight the specialness of the holiday by blessing the wine first).

We uncover the ḥallah before we recite the blessing. After the blessing we either cut or tear it—some people do not like to cut it because a knife can be used as a weapon and Shabbat is a time of peace. Traditionally, people sprinkle salt on the ḥallah before eating it. The table is considered to be an altar, and during the time of the ancient Temple in Jerusalem, salt was sprinkled on the offerings placed upon the altar there.

PRAYER DICTIONARY

Word Cards

Call on students individually to recite the introductory six words of a blessing, stopping after the word הָעוֹלָם. Display Word Cards 49–52 in random order. Choose one student to place the last four words of the blessing over bread in the correct order. Ask the class to recite the conclusion of the blessing in unison. (הַמּוֹצִיא לֶחֶם מִן הָאָרֶץ) Then, have students recite the English meaning of the blessing.

Who Brings Forth Bread from the Earth

- Does God bring forth *bread* from the earth? *(no)*

- What does God create and bring forth from the earth that we then use to create bread? *(wheat)*

- What other blessings has God given to us that we then use to create good for our world? *(foods that grow from the earth; medicines that are created from natural plants; cotton for clothing; wood for building homes)*

WORD MATCH

Direct students to complete the exercise individually. Call on students to recite a Shabbat blessing using each word in the exercise. *(blessing over bread)*

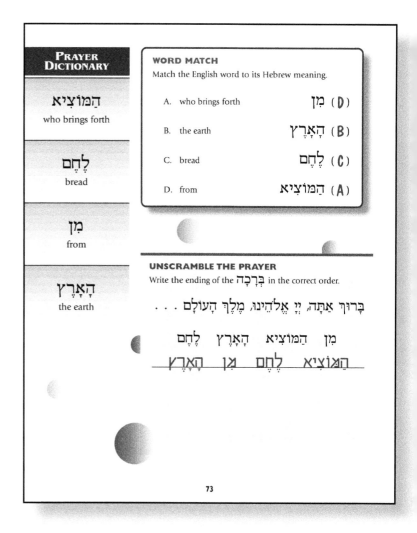

UNSCRAMBLE THE PRAYER

Display Word Cards 2, 4, 19, and 35–37 in the correct order. Place Word Cards 49–52 in scrambled order as found on the bottom of the page. While students do the unscrambling activity in their textbooks, call on one student to unscramble the Word Cards.

Blessing Review

Display Word Cards 42–52 in random order. Write the headings *Candles, Wine,* and *Bread* from right to left on the chalkboard. Have students select the appropriate Word Cards and post them under the heading that describes the blessing in which the words are used.

Challenge students to give the English meaning for each "blessing ending." Call on students to recite each complete blessing in Hebrew and English.

A Taste of Shabbat

Bring to class two Shabbat candlesticks and candles, grape juice (in place of wine) and a ḥallah, ḥallah cover, and a plate. Give each student a cup of grape juice. Cover the ḥallah. Perform the Shabbat rituals as students recite each blessing in turn. After the blessings are completed, share the food with the class.

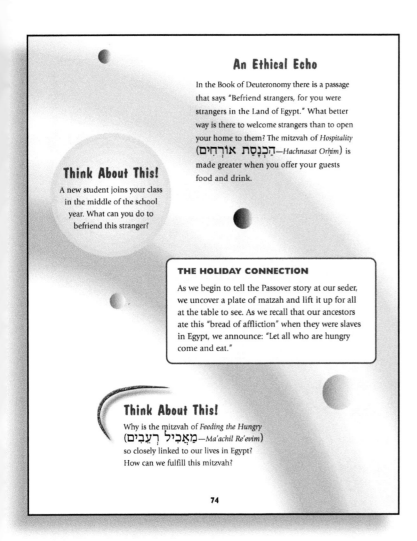

An Ethical Echo

In the Book of Deuteronomy there is a passage that says "Befriend strangers, for you were strangers in the Land of Egypt." What better way is there to welcome strangers than to open your home to them? The mitzvah of *Hospitality* (הַכְנָסַת אוֹרְחִים—*Hachnasat Orḥim*) is made greater when you offer your guests food and drink.

Think About This!

A new student joins your class in the middle of the school year. What can you do to befriend this stranger?

THE HOLIDAY CONNECTION

As we begin to tell the Passover story at our seder, we uncover a plate of matzah and lift it up for all at the table to see. As we recall that our ancestors ate this "bread of affliction" when they were slaves in Egypt, we announce: "Let all who are hungry come and eat."

Think About This!

Why is the mitzvah of *Feeding the Hungry* (מַאֲכִיל רְעֵבִים—*Ma'achil Re'evim*) so closely linked to our lives in Egypt? How can we fulfill this mitzvah?

74

AN ETHICAL ECHO

Discuss times when students may have felt like outsiders or strangers. If they feel comfortable, encourage them to discuss their experiences and feelings in these situations.

THINK ABOUT THIS!

Develop a "Hospitality Hello" for all new students who enter your school. You might mail a welcome card, plan a party, present a song, or display a banner in the hallway.

THE HOLIDAY CONNECTION

Read this section aloud with students.

Introduce the phrase that begins the reading in the haggadah: הָא לַחְמָא עַנְיָא—"this is the bread of affliction." Bring enough haggadot to class so that all may read the passage from the haggadah together.

THINK ABOUT THIS!

Discuss this question with students. *(we were hungry when we were slaves in Egypt; our food was of poor quality; we can fulfill the mitzvah with a food drive, by volunteering at a food pantry or homeless shelter)*

Discussion

During the seder we recite the blessing over bread, plus a בְּרָכָה שֶׁל מִצְוָה over the matzah. Ask students: Why do you think we are commanded to eat matzah? *(to demonstrate that we remember our time of slavery and what our lives were like then; as a reminder that others are hungry today)*

הַבְדָּלָה

INTRODUCING הַבְדָּלָה

Once again we see how Jewish ritual gives form and content to a significant Jewish event. Bring the ritual items for the Havdalah ceremony to class: wine cup, spice box filled with spices (e.g., cloves or cinnamon sticks), and a braided candle with multiple wicks. Explain that these items are used in the ceremony separating Shabbat from the week to come. There is a blessing we say over each Havdalah item just as there is a blessing we say over each item used to welcome Shabbat on a Friday night.

Ask the students:

- What three ritual items are used to welcome Shabbat? (*candles; wine; ḥallah*) Ask students to recite the blessing for each item in unison. (See page 66.)

- What three ritual items are used when taking leave of Shabbat? (*candle; wine; spices*) How do the Shabbat candles differ from the Havdalah candle? (*for Shabbat we use two or more independent candles; for Havdalah we use one braided candle with multiple wicks*)

Why a Braided Candle?

The blessing over the candle says: "Creator of the fiery lights" (sometimes translated as "Creator of the lights of fire"). The rabbis determined that the Havdalah candle must have two or more wicks. It is acceptable to hold two independent candles together so that the wicks create one flame.

Read the introduction with the students. Explain that we recite the Havdalah blessings when there are three stars in the sky on Saturday night. The three stars indicate that Shabbat has ended. (Note: There is an official time in every city for the end of Shabbat.)

Reading Practice

Form your class into groups of three students each. Each student in the group should take a number: 1, 2, or 3. Ask each group to practice the Havdalah blessings.

- Student 1 recites the first blessing (wine) to the group.

הַבְדָּלָה

Do you remember how we welcome Shabbat into our homes? We say בְּרָכוֹת over candles, wine, and ḥallah. There's also a special way that we say goodbye to Shabbat—with the Havdalah blessings.

הַבְדָּלָה means "separation." When we say the Havdalah blessings over wine, sweet spices, and a special braided candle, we are separating the uniqueness of Shabbat from the rest of the week. These blessings thank God for allowing us to celebrate Shabbat and ask God to help us remember its holiness throughout the next six days.

Imagine how you feel on your birthday. It's a special day, when everyone gives you extra attention with gifts, good wishes, and cake. Even when it's over, you can keep that wonderful feeling with you all year long by looking at photos or watching a video of your birthday party. It's the same with הַבְדָּלָה—the scent of the sweet spices and the bright light of the candle help us keep the Shabbat feeling with us all week long.

Practice reading the blessings over the wine, the spices, and the lit candle.

בָּרוּךְ אַתָּה, יְיָ אֱלֹהֵינוּ, מֶלֶךְ הָעוֹלָם, בּוֹרֵא פְּרִי הַגָּפֶן.
Praised are You, Adonai our God, Ruler of the world, who creates the fruit of the vine.

בָּרוּךְ אַתָּה, יְיָ אֱלֹהֵינוּ, מֶלֶךְ הָעוֹלָם, בּוֹרֵא מִינֵי בְשָׂמִים.
Praised are You, Adonai our God, Ruler of the world, who creates the varieties of spice.

בָּרוּךְ אַתָּה, יְיָ אֱלֹהֵינוּ, מֶלֶךְ הָעוֹלָם, בּוֹרֵא מְאוֹרֵי הָאֵשׁ.
Praised are You, Adonai our God, Ruler of the world, who creates the fiery lights.

75

- Student 2 recites the second blessing (spices) to the group.

- Student 3 recites the third blessing (lights) to the group.

Ask each group to repeat the activity two more times while changing the blessing each individual recites. This way each group member will have the opportunity to recite each blessing.

Direct all #1 students from each group to one area of the room, all #2 students from each group to a different area of the room, and all #3 students to a third area of the room.

- Call on Group 1 to recite the first blessing (wine) and its English meaning in unison.

- Call on Group 2 to recite the second blessing (spices) and its English meaning in unison.

- Call on Group 3 to recite the third blessing (lights) and its English meaning in unison.

If there is time, ask each group to repeat the activity saying a different blessing. This way each group will have the opportunity to recite each of the blessings.

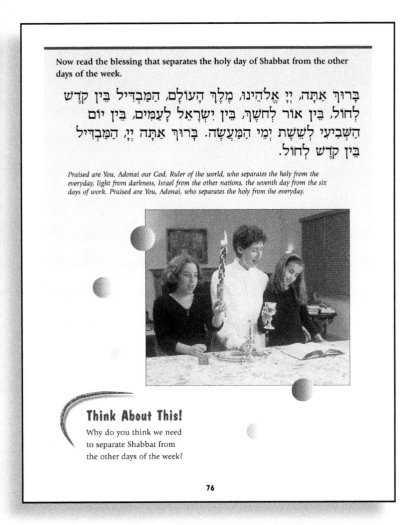

Now read the blessing that separates the holy day of Shabbat from the other days of the week.

בָּרוּךְ אַתָּה, יְיָ אֱלֹהֵינוּ, מֶלֶךְ הָעוֹלָם, הַמַּבְדִּיל בֵּין קֹדֶשׁ לְחוֹל, בֵּין אוֹר לְחֹשֶׁךְ, בֵּין יִשְׂרָאֵל לָעַמִּים, בֵּין יוֹם הַשְּׁבִיעִי לְשֵׁשֶׁת יְמֵי הַמַּעֲשֶׂה. בָּרוּךְ אַתָּה יְיָ, הַמַּבְדִּיל בֵּין קֹדֶשׁ לְחוֹל.

Praised are You, Adonai our God, Ruler of the world, who separates the holy from the everyday, light from darkness, Israel from the other nations, the seventh day from the six days of work. Praised are You, Adonai, who separates the holy from the everyday.

Think About This!

Why do you think we need to separate Shabbat from the other days of the week?

76

Havdalah Ritual

Model the Havdalah ceremony with students or consider inviting families to the class for a Havdalah ceremony. Have the students stand in a circle. Turn off the lights. Light the Havdalah candle.

- Ask the class to recite or sing the blessing over wine. (Use grape juice.) Wait to sip the grape juice until after the blessing of separation (page 76) which concludes the Havdalah ritual.

- Ask the class to recite or sing the blessing over spices. Shake the spice box and pass it around so all can inhale the sweet aroma of the spices.

- Ask the class to recite or sing the blessing over the lights. Traditionally, we cup our hands and extend our palms upward toward the lights of the candle.

- Ask the class to recite the blessing separating the holiness of Shabbat from the other days of the week. Sip the grape juice. Extinguish the candle in the remaining juice.

Read the Blessing

Read the introductory sentence with students. Read the English meaning following the blessing. Ask the class:

- For what "separations" does the blessing praise God? (*the holy from the everyday; light from darkness; Israel from the other nations; the seventh day from the six days of work*)

- Which "separation" is repeated at the beginning and the conclusion of the blessing? (*the holy from the everyday*)

Hebrew Reading

- Ask the class to recite the six-word blessing introduction. (בָּרוּךְ through הָעוֹלָם)

- Ask one student to recite the first "separation." (הַמַּבְדִּיל בֵּין קֹדֶשׁ לְחוֹל) (*who separates the holy from the everyday*)

- Ask a second student to recite the second "separation." (בֵּין אוֹר לְחֹשֶׁךְ) (*light from darkness*)

- Ask a third student to recite the third "separation." (בֵּין יִשְׂרָאֵל לָעַמִּים) (*the people of Israel from the other nations*)

- Ask a fourth student to recite the fourth "separation." (בֵּין יוֹם הַשְּׁבִיעִי לְשֵׁשֶׁת יְמֵי הַמַּעֲשֶׂה) (*the seventh day from the six days of work*)

Photo Op

Explain to the class that the elegant Havdalah ritual items reflect the tradition of הִדּוּר מִצְוָה— "beautifying the mitzvah."

THINK ABOUT THIS!

Read the question to the students. Discuss what makes Shabbat different from the other six days of the week. (*a day of rest from school; time to refresh ourselves; a change of pace; a day to give thanks for all we have*)

FLUENT READING

Direct students to find the following:

- words they know in each sentence—ask them to read the Hebrew and say the English meaning
- words built on the roots מ ל כ, ב ר כ, א ה ב, ק ד ש
- words ending with a final letter

Personal Best

Ask students to select five of the ten sentences and to practice them quietly. Then, call on students to try for a "personal best" by reading their selections two times each. Which of the two times was their better reading—their "personal best"?

Variation

Time the students with a stopwatch each of the two times. Which was the "personal best" reading time?

WORKSHEET (2)

Duplicate the worksheets for Lesson 7 to review rituals welcoming Shabbat and taking leave of Shabbat.

FAMILY EDUCATION

Begin planning for a Family Shabbat Dinner to be held at the conclusion of Lesson 9. Create a Shabbat Handbook with the blessings in Hebrew and the English translations. (Consider whether you want to include transliteration. Transliteration assists parents who do not read Hebrew and encourages their active participation.) Ask your students for explanations of the significance of each ritual and its blessing, and include those explanations in the handbook. Conclude the handbook with a student explanation of the Havdalah ceremony as well as the Havdalah blessings.

You can reduce the workload for this program by dividing the class into three groups. Assign Shabbat candlelighting to one group, the blessing over wine to a second group, and the blessing over bread to a third. Have group members discuss and formulate an explanation of the assigned ritual for inclusion in the handbook, and ask each group to present their explanations to the class for further input. Use

---

FLUENT READING

Practice reading the lines below.

1. וְשַׁבַּת קָדְשׁוֹ בְּאַהֲבָה וּבְרָצוֹן הִנְחִילָנוּ.

2. וְשָׁמְרוּ בְנֵי יִשְׂרָאֵל אֶת הַשַּׁבָּת, לַעֲשׂוֹת אֶת הַשַּׁבָּת לְדֹרֹתָם.

3. בָּרוּךְ אַתָּה, יְיָ אֱלֹהֵינוּ, מֶלֶךְ הָעוֹלָם, עֹשֵׂה מַעֲשֵׂה בְרֵאשִׁית.

4. בְּרֵאשִׁית בָּרָא אֱלֹהִים אֵת הַשָּׁמַיִם וְאֵת הָאָרֶץ.

5. אֲדוֹן הַשָּׁלוֹם, מְקַדֵּשׁ הַשַּׁבָּת וּמְבָרֵךְ שְׁבִיעִי.

6. בָּרוּךְ אַתָּה יְיָ, מֶלֶךְ עַל כָּל הָאָרֶץ.

7. מְקַדֵּשׁ יִשְׂרָאֵל וְיוֹם הַזִּכָּרוֹן.

8. זִכָּרוֹן לְמַעֲשֵׂה בְרֵאשִׁית.

9. טוֹבִים מְאוֹרוֹת שֶׁבָּרָא אֱלֹהֵינוּ.

10. בָּרוּךְ אַתָּה, יְיָ אֱלֹהֵינוּ, מֶלֶךְ הָעוֹלָם, אֲשֶׁר קִדְּשָׁנוּ בְּמִצְוֹתָיו וְצִוָּנוּ לְהַדְלִיק נֵר שֶׁל שַׁבָּת.

77

the same three groups to develop the Havdalah ceremony for inclusion in the handbook.

They will expand the handbook at the conclusion of Lesson 9.

Families may not be knowledgeable about the significance of Shabbat rituals. Send students home with the "As a Family: Celebrating Shabbat" page (at the back of this guide) to familiarize them with the significance of the three Shabbat blessings and rituals: over candles, over wine, over bread.

Name: _____

בְּרָכוֹת שֶׁל שַׁבָּת

1. Unscramble the ending for each blessing we recite to welcome Shabbat. Then complete the English meaning of each blessing.

   Candlelighting:

   בָּרוּךְ אַתָּה, יְיָ אֱלֹהֵינוּ, מֶלֶךְ הָעוֹלָם _____
   _____

   וְצִוָּנוּ / נֵר / קִדְּשָׁנוּ / לְהַדְלִיק / אֲשֶׁר / שַׁבָּת / שֶׁל / בְּמִצְוֹתָיו

   Praised are You, Adonai our God, Ruler of the world _____
   _____

   Wine:

   בָּרוּךְ אַתָּה, יְיָ אֱלֹהֵינוּ, מֶלֶךְ הָעוֹלָם _____

   פְּרִי / בּוֹרֵא / הַגָּפֶן

   Praised are You, Adonai our God, Ruler of the world
   _____

   Bread:

   בָּרוּךְ אַתָּה, יְיָ אֱלֹהֵינוּ, מֶלֶךְ הָעוֹלָם _____

   הָאָרֶץ / הַמּוֹצִיא / מִן / לֶחֶם

   Praised are You, Adonai our God, Ruler of the world
   _____
   _____

2. Which of the three בְּרָכוֹת is a בְּרָכָה שֶׁל מִצְוָה? _____

3. Explain the symbolism of each ritual.

   Candlelighting: _____

   Wine: _____

Name: _____

הַבְדָּלָה

1. Unscramble the ending for each blessing we recite in the הַבְדָּלָה ceremony. Then complete the English meaning of each blessing.

   Wine:

   בָּרוּךְ אַתָּה, יְיָ אֱלֹהֵינוּ, מֶלֶךְ הָעוֹלָם _____

   _____

   הַגָּפֶן / בּוֹרֵא / פְּרִי

   Praised are You, Adonai our God, Ruler of the world
   _____

   _____

   Spices:

   בָּרוּךְ אַתָּה, יְיָ אֱלֹהֵינוּ, מֶלֶךְ הָעוֹלָם _____

   מִינֵי / בְשָׂמִים / בּוֹרֵא

   Praised are You, Adonai our God, Ruler of the world
   _____

   _____

   Havdalah Candle:

   בָּרוּךְ אַתָּה, יְיָ אֱלֹהֵינוּ, מֶלֶךְ הָעוֹלָם _____

   בּוֹרֵא / הָאֵשׁ / מְאוֹרֵי

   Praised are You, Adonai our God, Ruler of the world
   _____

   _____

   What is the meaning of the word בּוֹרֵא in each blessing?

   _____

2. When does the הַבְדָּלָה ceremony take place? _____

3. What does the word הַבְדָּלָה mean? _____

LESSON 8

בְּרָכוֹת שֶׁל יוֹם טוֹב

LEARNING OBJECTIVES

Prayer Reading Skills

Term: יוֹם טוֹב (literally, "a good day"; a Jewish holiday—חָג)

Blessings for:

Rosh Hashanah

Sukkot

Ḥanukkah

Pesaḥ

Prayer Concepts

Holiday traditions for:

Rosh Hashanah: dipping apples in honey; hearing the sounds of the shofar

Sukkot: eating in the sukkah as a remembrance of the way our ancestors lived in the wilderness

Ḥanukkah: a time of miracles

Pesaḥ: symbolism of matzah; Passover seder

Ethical Echo: Freedom

INTRODUCING THE PRAYER

Each יוֹם טוֹב—Jewish holiday—has its own traditions and its own blessings. The traditions connect us to our past while at the same time we celebrate in the present and look ahead to the future. The blessings we recite are an expression of our appreciation for all the good that has come our way.

INSTRUCTIONAL MATERIALS

Text pages 78–85

Word Cards 47 and 53–64

Worksheet for Lesson 8

Family Education: "As a Family: The Miracle of Ḥanukkah" (at the back of this guide)

CYCLE OF TIME

Recognizing Ritual Items

Display holiday ritual items in random order on a table:

- Rosh Hashanah: apples and honey, a shofar, a maḥzor
- Sukkot: a model sukkah, a picture of a sukkah, a picture of a lulav and etrog, harvest foods
- Ḥanukkah: a ḥanukkiyah (Ḥanukkah menorah), dreidels, gelt, oil, potatoes
- Pesaḥ: matzah, a seder plate, salt water, wine, a haggadah

On a second table display signs designating each holiday: Rosh Hashanah, Sukkot, Ḥanukkah, Pesaḥ.

Call on individual students to place the ritual items next to the correct holiday name thus creating a class display. Ask students to suggest a label for the display. (*Our Jewish Year; The Cycle of Time; Jewish Time*)

Discuss with students:

- the symbolism of each of the ritual items
- how they celebrate each holiday at home and in the synagogue

Extending the Discussion

What other holidays do we celebrate in our calendar cycle? (*Shavuot, Yom Kippur, Simḥat Torah*) What are the ritual or traditional items for these holidays? (*Shavuot: Ten Commandments*, Sefer Torah, *flowers, dairy products, first fruits; Yom Kippur: white clothing, shofar, maḥzor; Simḥat Torah:* Sefer Torah, *flags, apples*)

בְּרָכוֹת שֶׁל יוֹם טוֹב ⑧

Just as there are special בְּרָכוֹת for the things we are grateful for during the week and on Shabbat, there are also special blessings for the Jewish holidays.

From Rosh Hashanah and Yom Kippur, to Sukkot, Simḥat Torah, Ḥanukkah, Purim, Pesaḥ and more, each Jewish holiday—יוֹם טוֹב—has its own wonderful way of saying "thank you" to God.

What are some of the בְּרָכוֹת for the holidays?

ROSH HASHANAH

On Rosh Hashanah, we ask God for a sweet new year by dipping slices of apple into honey while saying the בְּרָכָה for fruit. We also say a בְּרָכָה just before we blow or hear the Shofar.

Practice reading these blessings recited on Rosh Hashanah.
Read the Hebrew name for each of the holiday objects pictured.

1. בָּרוּךְ אַתָּה, יְיָ אֱלֹהֵינוּ, מֶלֶךְ הָעוֹלָם,
בּוֹרֵא פְּרִי הָעֵץ.

*Praised are You, Adonai our God, Ruler of the world,
who creates the fruit of the tree.*

תַּפּוּחַ דְּבַשׁ

2. בָּרוּךְ אַתָּה, יְיָ אֱלֹהֵינוּ, מֶלֶךְ הָעוֹלָם,
אֲשֶׁר קִדְּשָׁנוּ בְּמִצְוֹתָיו
וְצִוָּנוּ לִשְׁמֹעַ קוֹל שׁוֹפָר.

*Praised are You, Adonai our God, Ruler of the world,
who makes us holy with commandments, and commands us
to hear the sound of the shofar.*

שׁוֹפָר

78

ROSH HASHANAH

Read the introduction with students.

Read the paragraph introducing the blessings.

Apples and Honey

Bring apples and honey to class. Ask each student to dip a slice of apple in the honey. Then ask students to recite the blessing together in Hebrew and in English, and to wish each other "a sweet, good year" (שָׁנָה טוֹבָה וּמְתוּקָה). Then, enjoy the snack. It is also a custom to dip ḥallah in the honey.

Sound of the Shofar

Explain: In Biblical times the shofar was used to call the people to attention or to action. Tradition says we heard the sound of the shofar just before God gave the Torah to the Jews at Mt. Sinai (Exodus 19:13, 16–19).

Direct students to the blessing.

- What phrase, in Hebrew and in English, tells us this is a בְּרָכָה שֶׁל מִצְוָה, a blessing of mitzvah? (אֲשֶׁר קִדְּשָׁנוּ בְּמִצְוֹתָיו וְצִוָּנוּ—*who makes us holy with commandments and commands us*)

- Call on each student to read the commandment (the last three words of the blessing) aloud.

- What are we commanded to do? (*to hear the sound of the shofar*)

- Which Hebrew word means "to hear"? Hint: Think of the שְׁמַע. (לִשְׁמֹעַ)

- Read the blessing in unison.

Bring a shofar to class. Explain the different sounds of the shofar—*Tekiah*: one long, clear blast; *Sh'varim*: a set of three short blasts; *Teru'ah*: a row of nine very short blasts; *Tekiah Gedolah* ("great *tekiah*"): one very long blast coming at the end of a series of shofar calls.

If possible, invite someone to class who can blow a shofar. Have the class recite the blessing before the blowing of the shofar.

PRAYER DICTIONARY

Word Cards

Display Word Cards 47 and 53. Ask for the English meaning of each one. Then ask students to recite the blessing over the fruit of the tree without looking back at page 78.

Display Word Card 54. Read it aloud. Challenge each student to give one fact about the shofar.

Direct students to complete the exercises on the page individually.

SEARCH AND CIRCLE

Allow students a few moments to complete the exercise. Challenge students to give the meaning of the words that are not circled. *(right to left line 1: one, you; line 2: hear, Israel; line 3: candle, ruler)*

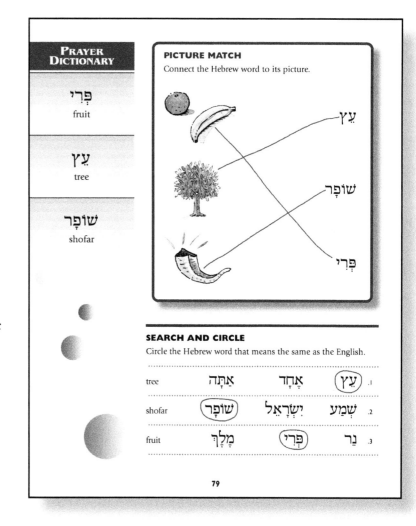

SUKKOT

On Sukkot, we say a בְּרָכָה when we eat our meals in the sukkah. We remember how our ancestors wandered through the wilderness for forty years before reaching the Land of Israel, living in huts while God provided them with food. When we look up through the branches that form the roof of a sukkah, we can see the same stars our ancestors saw!

Practice reading the בְּרָכָה we say in the sukkah.

בָּרוּךְ אַתָּה, יְיָ אֱלֹהֵינוּ, מֶלֶךְ הָעוֹלָם, אֲשֶׁר
קִדְּשָׁנוּ בְּמִצְוֹתָיו וְצִוָּנוּ לֵישֵׁב בַּסֻּכָּה.

Praised are You, Adonai our God, Ruler of the world, who makes us holy with commandments and commands us to sit in the sukkah.

Practice reading the בְּרָכָה we say when shaking the lulav.

בָּרוּךְ אַתָּה, יְיָ אֱלֹהֵינוּ, מֶלֶךְ הָעוֹלָם, אֲשֶׁר
קִדְּשָׁנוּ בְּמִצְוֹתָיו וְצִוָּנוּ עַל נְטִילַת לוּלָב.

Praised are You, Adonai our God, Ruler of the world, who makes us holy with commandments and commands us to shake the lulav.

80

SUKKOT

Read the introduction with students.

Direct students to the first blessing. Ask them:

- What phrase, in Hebrew and in English, tells us this is a בְּרָכָה שֶׁל מִצְוָה, a blessing of mitzvah? (אֲשֶׁר קִדְּשָׁנוּ בְּמִצְוֹתָיו וְצִוָּנוּ —*who makes us holy with commandments and commands us*)

- To read the commandment (the last two words of the blessing) aloud.

- What are we commanded to do? (*to sit in the sukkah*)

Display Word Card 55. Ask students to read the word in unison. Then ask them for the meaning of the word. (A hint: Look at the blessing ending.) Read the blessing in unison.

Direct the class to the second blessing. Ask them to read the entire blessing in unison, and then call on individual students to do so. Ask them: What are we commanded to do? (*shake the lulav*)

Extending the Discussion

It is a custom to "invite" special Biblical guests known as *ushpizin* to join us in the sukkah. Traditionally, we invited Abraham, Isaac, Jacob, Joseph, Moses, Aaron, and David. Today we also invite women from the Bible or other famous Jewish figures. Whom would you invite? (*Sarah, Rebecca, Leah, Rachel, Miriam, Esther, Deborah . . .*)

It is a tradition to welcome friends, relatives, and neighbors into the sukkah to eat with us. Whom would you invite today?

Photo Op

Where is the girl standing? (*in a sukkah*) What is she holding? (*a lulav and etrog*) The lulav and the etrog remind us of the many things that grow from the earth.

- The etrog is a citron. It looks like a large, bumpy lemon. It has a delicate, fresh aroma.

- The lulav consists of the branches of a palm tree (lulav), a leafy tree (myrtle), and a willow. The branches are bundled together. The tall palm branch is in the middle. On one side are three myrtle branches and on the other side are two willow branches. The bundle is called a lulav because the lulav is the tallest part.

ḤANUKKAH

Read the introduction with the students.

Practice Reading

Direct students to the first blessing. Read it in unison. Then:

- Ask the class what phrase, in Hebrew and in English, tells us this is a בְּרָכָה שֶׁל מִצְוָה, a blessing of mitzvah.

אֲשֶׁר קִדְּשָׁנוּ בְּמִצְוֹתָיו וְצִוָּנוּ)
—who makes us holy with commandments and commands us)

- Call on each student to read the commandment (the last four words of the blessing) aloud.

- Ask the class what we are commanded to do. (*light the Ḥanukkah candles*)

- Read the blessing again in unison with the class.

Direct students to the second blessing.

- Display Word Cards 58 and 59 in turn. Call on students to read each word and give its English meaning. (Hint: Have students look at the Prayer Dictionary.) Direct students to circle each word and its English meaning in the blessing.

- Call on students to read the English meaning of the blessing aloud. Ask: What were the Ḥanukkah miracles at this season? (*victory of the Maccabees for religious freedom; oil lasting 8 days*)

- Allow students time to practice the blessing aloud with a partner.

- Ask the class to read the six-word introduction to the blessing (בָּרוּךְ-הָעוֹלָם) in unison. Then call on each student individually to read its conclusion (שֶׁעָשָׂה-הַזֶּה).

- Ask the entire class to read the entire blessing in unison.

To provide immediate reinforcement and to introduce the third blessing, have the class read the first two blessings in unison.

Then, read the introduction for the third blessing aloud to the class. Ask a student to read the English meaning of the blessing. Explain that we recite this blessing (the שֶׁהֶחֱיָנוּ) at the start of most holidays. We also recite this blessing at life-cycle events and on special occasions.

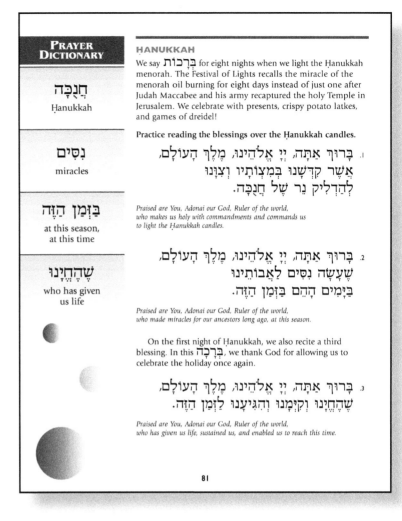

PRAYER DICTIONARY

חֲנֻכָּה
Ḥanukkah

נִסִּים
miracles

בַּזְּמַן הַזֶּה
at this season,
at this time

שֶׁהֶחֱיָנוּ
who has given
us life

ḤANUKKAH

We say בְּרָכוֹת for eight nights when we light the Ḥanukkah menorah. The Festival of Lights recalls the miracle of the menorah oil burning for eight days instead of just one after Judah Maccabee and his army recaptured the holy Temple in Jerusalem. We celebrate with presents, crispy potato latkes, and games of dreidel!

Practice reading the blessings over the Ḥanukkah candles.

1. בָּרוּךְ אַתָּה, יְיָ אֱלֹהֵינוּ, מֶלֶךְ הָעוֹלָם,
אֲשֶׁר קִדְּשָׁנוּ בְּמִצְוֹתָיו וְצִוָּנוּ
לְהַדְלִיק נֵר שֶׁל חֲנֻכָּה.

Praised are You, Adonai our God, Ruler of the world,
who makes us holy with commandments and commands us
to light the Ḥanukkah candles.

2. בָּרוּךְ אַתָּה, יְיָ אֱלֹהֵינוּ, מֶלֶךְ הָעוֹלָם,
שֶׁעָשָׂה נִסִּים לַאֲבוֹתֵינוּ
בַּיָּמִים הָהֵם בַּזְּמַן הַזֶּה.

Praised are You, Adonai our God, Ruler of the world,
who made miracles for our ancestors long ago, at this season.

On the first night of Ḥanukkah, we also recite a third blessing. In this בְּרָכָה, we thank God for allowing us to celebrate the holiday once again.

3. בָּרוּךְ אַתָּה, יְיָ אֱלֹהֵינוּ, מֶלֶךְ הָעוֹלָם,
שֶׁהֶחֱיָנוּ וְקִיְּמָנוּ וְהִגִּיעָנוּ לַזְּמַן הַזֶּה.

Praised are You, Adonai our God, Ruler of the world,
who has given us life, sustained us, and enabled us to reach this time.

81

Reading Skills

Display Word Card 60. Have the class read it aloud. Ask for the English meaning. Then have the students circle the Hebrew word and its English meaning in the blessing.

Recite the third blessing with the class. Recite all three blessings over again. If you are comfortable, practice chanting the blessings with the students.

WORD MATCH

Connect the Hebrew to its English meaning.

at this season, at this time   נִסִּים

Hanukkah   שֶׁהֶחֱיָנוּ

miracles   חֲנֻכָּה

who has given us life   בַּזְּמָן הַזֶּה

HOLIDAY DRAWINGS

Read the names of the holidays.
What objects do *you* use to celebrate each one?
Draw or list your favorite holiday objects.

_____ רֹאשׁ הַשָּׁנָה

_____ סֻכּוֹת

_____ שִׂמְחַת תּוֹרָה

_____ חֲנֻכָּה

_____ פּוּרִים

_____ פֶּסַח

82

An Ethical Echo

Judah Maccabee led a revolt for religious freedom. But religious freedom isn't the only kind of freedom (חֵרוּת) people require to live full, happy lives. What other kinds of freedom do people need?

Think About This!

Can you think of other times when Jews were *not* free? Can you think of other people from the Bible who risked their lives so that the Jewish people could live freely?

AN ETHICAL ECHO

Read the "Ethical Echo" aloud with students. Develop a list of other kinds of freedoms needed to live happy lives. (*Freedom from: illness; hunger; poverty; homelessness; bigotry; anger. Freedom to: practice our religion; express ourselves without fear of reprisal; travel freely; have privacy*) Discuss with students what actions they might take to help people be free. (*food drives; visits, calls, and cards to people in need of companionship; holiday and birthday toy drives*)

THINK ABOUT THIS!

Think about times in Jewish history when Jews were persecuted or not allowed the freedom to live in the land of Israel. (*Babylonian conquest; Roman conquest; the Holocaust; wars in the Middle East*) Review stories from the Bible of those who risked their lives for our freedom. (*Moses, Aaron, Joshua, Esther*)

PESAḤ

Read the introduction aloud with students.

Display Word Cards 61–64. Call on students individually to read each word. As they read the word, ask them to give the English meaning. Then, have the class circle the word and its English meaning in their textbooks.

Note: The word אֲכִילַת is in the blessing for matzah *and* bitter herbs.

בְּרָכוֹת שֶׁל מִצְוָה

- Read the blessings that are בְּרָכוֹת שֶׁל מִצְוָה. *(the last two)* Ask the class: How do we know these are בְּרָכוֹת שֶׁל מִצְוָה? *(the phrase* אֲשֶׁר קִדְּשָׁנוּ בְּמִצְוֹתָיו וְצִוָּנוּ—*who makes us holy with commandments and commands us)*

- Call on individual students to read each commandment (the last three words of the last two blessings) aloud.

- Ask the class: What are we commanded to do? *(eat matzah; eat bitter herbs)*

Call on students to read all five blessings in turn. Make sure they say the English meaning after each Hebrew blessing.

Blessing Questions

Discuss the practice of the holiday with your students by asking them the following questions:

- Do you remember how many cups of wine we drink at the seder? *(four)* Why do we drink four cups of wine? *(to represent four of God's promises: I will free you; I will deliver you; I will redeem you; I will take you to be My people [Exodus 6:6–7])* Note: The Cup of Elijah filled with wine represents God's fifth promise, filled with hope but not yet fulfilled at the time of the Exodus: "and I will bring you into the land" (Exodus 6:8).

- What does the green vegetable represent? *(springtime; new beginnings both in nature and for our people when we were freed from slavery)*

- Why do we recite the blessing over bread at Pesaḥ? *(matzah is the bread of Pesaḥ; the blessing over bread represents all the food on the table—see text page 72)*

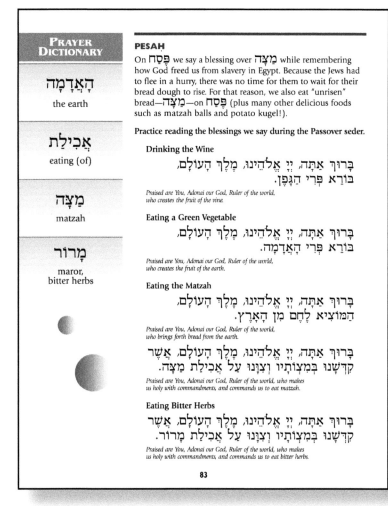

- Why do we praise God for commanding us to eat matzah? *(we praise God for commanding the actions that help us remember our history and our flight to freedom)*

- Why do we praise God for commanding us to eat bitter herbs? *(so that we can symbolically understand the bitterness of our lives and what bitter lives mean to others, encouraging us to take action to help them)*

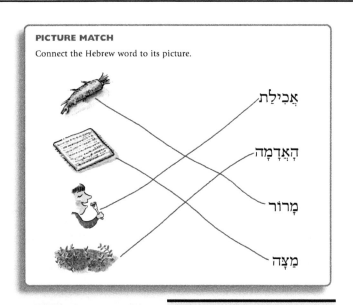

PICTURE MATCH

Ask students to connect the words to the pictures.

FILL IN THE BLANK

Have students look at the two בְּרָכוֹת שֶׁל מִצְוָה on page 83 for the correct spelling of the missing word. Call on students to recite each complete blessing. Review the symbolism of matzah and maror.

Photo Op

Ask: What items on the Passover table and seder plate do you recognize? Call on students to recite the blessing for each item they name. (See page 83 for the blessings.)

FLUENT READING

Which two phrases are not בְּרָכוֹת שֶׁל מִצְוָה?
(*1 and 5*) Recite each one.

Which phrases are בְּרָכוֹת שֶׁל מִצְוָה?
(*2, 3, 4, 6, 7, 8*) Recite each one.

Review the occasions on which we say each blessing.
(*1: holidays and special occasions; 2: over the holiday
candles; 3: Purim, upon reading the Megillah; 4:
Passover before eating matzah; 5: before eating fruit
from a tree; 6: lighting the Ḥanukkah candles; 7:
Passover before eating bitter herbs; 8: Sukkot when
waving the lulav*)

Blessing Line

Divide the class into two groups; ask each group
to line up facing you. Pick a group to go first,
describe a blessing (e.g., "we recite this blessing
before lighting the Ḥanukkah candles"), and ask
the first player in the line to recite the blessing.
Then the next group goes. Continue until each
student has had a turn.

WORKSHEET

Duplicate Worksheet 8 to review holiday blessings.

FAMILY EDUCATION

Duplicate and send home with students the
Family Education page "As a Family: The Miracle
of Ḥanukkah" (at the back of this guide).

FLUENT READING

Practice reading these holiday blessings. Do you know when we say each one?

1. בָּרוּךְ אַתָּה, יְיָ אֱלֹהֵינוּ, מֶלֶךְ הָעוֹלָם,
שֶׁהֶחֱיָנוּ וְקִיְּמָנוּ וְהִגִּיעָנוּ לַזְּמַן הַזֶּה.

2. בָּרוּךְ אַתָּה, יְיָ אֱלֹהֵינוּ, מֶלֶךְ הָעוֹלָם,
אֲשֶׁר קִדְּשָׁנוּ בְּמִצְוֹתָיו וְצִוָּנוּ לְהַדְלִיק נֵר שֶׁל יוֹם טוֹב.

3. בָּרוּךְ אַתָּה, יְיָ אֱלֹהֵינוּ, מֶלֶךְ הָעוֹלָם,
אֲשֶׁר קִדְּשָׁנוּ בְּמִצְוֹתָיו וְצִוָּנוּ עַל מִקְרָא מְגִלָּה.

4. בָּרוּךְ אַתָּה, יְיָ אֱלֹהֵינוּ, מֶלֶךְ הָעוֹלָם,
אֲשֶׁר קִדְּשָׁנוּ בְּמִצְוֹתָיו וְצִוָּנוּ עַל אֲכִילַת מַצָּה.

5. בָּרוּךְ אַתָּה, יְיָ אֱלֹהֵינוּ, מֶלֶךְ הָעוֹלָם,
בּוֹרֵא פְּרִי הָעֵץ.

6. בָּרוּךְ אַתָּה, יְיָ אֱלֹהֵינוּ, מֶלֶךְ הָעוֹלָם,
אֲשֶׁר קִדְּשָׁנוּ בְּמִצְוֹתָיו וְצִוָּנוּ לְהַדְלִיק נֵר שֶׁל חֲנֻכָּה.

7. בָּרוּךְ אַתָּה, יְיָ אֱלֹהֵינוּ, מֶלֶךְ הָעוֹלָם,
אֲשֶׁר קִדְּשָׁנוּ בְּמִצְוֹתָיו וְצִוָּנוּ עַל אֲכִילַת מָרוֹר.

8. בָּרוּךְ אַתָּה, יְיָ אֱלֹהֵינוּ, מֶלֶךְ הָעוֹלָם,
אֲשֶׁר קִדְּשָׁנוּ בְּמִצְוֹתָיו וְצִוָּנוּ עַל נְטִילַת לוּלָב.

85

בְּרָכוֹת שֶׁל יוֹם טוֹב

1. Write the English next to each Hebrew word.

4. נִסִּים _____		1. מַצָּה _____	
5. עֵץ _____		2. שׁוֹפָר _____	
6. פְּרִי _____		3. הָאֲדָמָה _____	

2. The following phrases are blessing endings. Write the Hebrew name of the holiday next to the matching blessing ending.

סֻכּוֹת   פּוּרִים   חֲנֻכָּה   פֶּסַח   ראֹשׁ הַשָּׁנָה

1. עַל אֲכִילַת מַצָּה _____

2. לִשְׁמֹעַ קוֹל שׁוֹפָר _____

3. לֵישֵׁב בַּסֻּכָּה _____

4. שֶׁעָשָׂה נִסִּים לַאֲבוֹתֵינוּ _____
בַּיָּמִים הָהֵם בַּזְּמַן הַזֶּה

5. עַל אֲכִילַת מָרוֹר _____

6. עַל מִקְרָא מְגִלָּה _____

7. עַל-נְטִילַת לוּלָב _____

3. Describe the miracles to explain the blessing ending:

שֶׁעָשָׂה נִסִּים לַאֲבוֹתֵינוּ בַּיָּמִים הָהֵם בַּזְּמַן הַזֶּה

_____

_____

_____

LESSON קִדּוּשׁ 9

LEARNING OBJECTIVES

Prayer Reading Skills

Reading the Kiddush

Root: ז כ ר ("memory," "remember")

Review Root: ק ד שׁ ("holy")

Prayer Concepts

The קִדּוּשׁ begins with the blessing over wine.

The קִדּוּשׁ is recited twice on Friday night: in the synagogue and in the home.

We are a holy people.

Performing mitzvot adds holiness to our lives.

Memory is important to the Jewish people:

> The קִדּוּשׁ helps us remember the work of creation.

> The קִדּוּשׁ helps us remember our going forth from Egypt.

INTRODUCING THE PRAYER

The Hebrew word קִדּוּשׁ means "sanctification." In the Torah we are commanded to "remember the Sabbath day and keep it holy" (Exodus 20:8), and one of the ways we perform this commandment is by reciting the קִדּוּשׁ. Shabbat is a time of joy ("If you call the Sabbath a joy, God's holy day is honored" [Isaiah 58:13]), and wine is a symbol of joy ("Wine makes glad the human heart" [Psalm 104:15]), and so we recite קִדּוּשׁ with wine on Shabbat.

INSTRUCTIONAL MATERIALS

Text pages 86–95

Word Cards 65–71

Worksheet for Lesson 9

Family Education: "As a Family: Remembering Creation and Freedom" (at the back of this guide)

SET INDUCTION

The קִדּוּשׁ is about memory—the memory of creation and the memory of our going out from Egypt. Highlight for students the importance of memory: Ask them to recall one or two events in their lives that were unique and had an important influence on them. Encourage them to discuss these events and how they were affected. *(birth of a baby in the family; death of a relative; special trip; moving to a new home; grandparent coming to live with the family)*

Now have the class think back upon a special collective memory—something they have experienced as part of the Jewish community, or as part of the religious school, or as part of the class. *(Possible responses: schoolwide holiday event; commemoration service for Yom Hashoah; reading about and identifying with resettlement of Jews from other lands; a trip to Israel)* Again encourage students to discuss how they were affected.

The Memory of Creation:

Review the story of creation: Genesis 1:1–2:4. Why is it important that we stop to remember creation each Shabbat? *(to show appreciation of the world; to make time for reflecting upon what we can do to improve the world)*

The Memory of Our Exodus from Egypt:

Review the story of our going forth from Egypt. We are told in the haggadah to think of ourselves as if each one of us went out from Egypt, as if each one of us has not only a collective memory of the Exodus, but an individual memory as well. Why do we have this obligation? *(to recognize that God redeemed each one of us, and that is why we are free to be Jews today; to realize that we were freed to receive God's Torah; so that we will each understand what slavery means and will seek ways to free others who are enslaved or oppressed)*

קִדּוּשׁ ⟨9⟩

Do you remember that the קִדּוּשׁ is one of the בְּרָכוֹת we say to welcome and sanctify Shabbat? We also say it on many holidays, including Rosh Hashanah, Sukkot, and Pesaḥ. The קִדּוּשׁ separates these occasions from the everyday and helps us to make them holy.

The קִדּוּשׁ begins with the blessing over the wine, thanking God for creating the fruit of the vine—the grapes from which we make wine.

The קִדּוּשׁ for Shabbat reminds us that we were chosen by God with love to observe Shabbat and to carry out God's commandments.

The קִדּוּשׁ begins with a בְּרָכָה you have already learned.

בָּרוּךְ אַתָּה, יְיָ אֱלֹהֵינוּ, מֶלֶךְ הָעוֹלָם, בּוֹרֵא פְּרִי הַגָּפֶן.

Can you say this בְּרָכָה by heart?

Practice reading the קִדּוּשׁ for Shabbat aloud.

1. בָּרוּךְ אַתָּה, יְיָ אֱלֹהֵינוּ, מֶלֶךְ הָעוֹלָם, בּוֹרֵא פְּרִי הַגָּפֶן.
2. בָּרוּךְ אַתָּה, יְיָ אֱלֹהֵינוּ, מֶלֶךְ הָעוֹלָם, אֲשֶׁר קִדְּשָׁנוּ
3. בְּמִצְוֹתָיו וְרָצָה בָנוּ, וְשַׁבַּת קָדְשׁוֹ בְּאַהֲבָה וּבְרָצוֹן
4. הִנְחִילָנוּ, זִכָּרוֹן לְמַעֲשֵׂה בְרֵאשִׁית. כִּי הוּא יוֹם תְּחִלָּה
5. לְמִקְרָאֵי קֹדֶשׁ, זֵכֶר לִיצִיאַת מִצְרָיִם. כִּי בָנוּ בָחַרְתָּ
6. וְאוֹתָנוּ קִדַּשְׁתָּ מִכָּל הָעַמִּים, וְשַׁבַּת קָדְשְׁךָ בְּאַהֲבָה
7. וּבְרָצוֹן הִנְחַלְתָּנוּ. בָּרוּךְ אַתָּה יְיָ, מְקַדֵּשׁ הַשַּׁבָּת.

Praised are You, Adonai our God, Ruler of the world, who creates the fruit of the vine.
Praised are You, Adonai our God, Ruler of the world, who makes us holy
with commandments and takes delight in us. In God's love and favor God has made the
holy Sabbath our heritage, as a memory of the work of creation.
It is first among our holy days, a memory of the going out from Egypt.
You chose us from all the nations and You made us holy, and in (with) love and favor You
have given us the Sabbath as a sacred inheritance.
Praised are You, Adonai, who makes the Sabbath holy.

86

INTO THE TEXT

Read the introductory paragraph with students. Call on students to read the blessing over wine in Hebrew (line 1) followed by the English translation.

Ask students to recite the ten Hebrew words that usually introduce a blessing of mitzvah (בָּרוּךְ . . . וְצִוָּנוּ). (Hint: See page 60.) What is the English translation of these ten words? (Hint: See page 60—*Praised are You, Adonai our God, Ruler of the world, who makes us holy with God's commandments and commands us . . .*")

For Discussion

Read the second English sentence ("Praised are You . . . takes delight in us"). What do we do that delights God? (*act in the image of God; follow God's teachings and commandments; welcome Shabbat; attend worship services*) Read the complete English translation. How do we demonstrate that we treasure Shabbat, our sacred inheritance? (*honor Shabbat with special rituals such as lighting Shabbat candles; acknowledge through our actions that Shabbat is different from the other six days of the week*)

Read the blessing over wine and the קִדּוּשׁ in unison with students.

PRAYER DICTIONARY

Word Cards

Hand out Word Cards 65–71 to seven different students. Tell students you will give clues to indicate a specific Word Card that you are looking for. The student holding that Word Card should identify it, then pass it to another student. Next, give another clue for the next Word Card. Repeat this process until every student has had a turn with a card. For the last round, students holding correct cards should display them on the edge of the chalkboard instead of passing them to another student. (You can expand the game by including Word Cards from previous lessons as well.)

Sample Clues

You can make your own clues. Some starter clues are:

- Write the root ז כ ר on the chalkboard. Say: "I am looking for the two words meaning 'memory.'" Both words are built on this root. (זָכֵר   זִכָּרוֹן)

- Write בְּרֵאשִׁית on the chalkboard. Say: "This is the Hebrew word meaning 'creation.' I am looking for the phrase meaning 'work of creation.'" (לְמַעֲשֵׂה בְּרֵאשִׁית)

- Write ק ד שׁ on the chalkboard. Say, "I am looking for the word meaning 'making holy' or 'sanctification.' It is built on this root." (קָדוֹשׁ)

- Say, "I am looking for a phrase that represents our Exodus from slavery." ((לְ)יְצִיאַת מִצְרָיִם)

PRAYER DICTIONARY	
קָדוֹשׁ	sanctification
זִכָּרוֹן	memory
(לְ)מַעֲשֵׂה בְּרֵאשִׁית	work of creation
זֵכֶר	memory
(לְ)יְצִיאַת מִצְרָיִם	going out from Egypt
בְּאַהֲבָה	in (with) love
וּבְרָצוֹן	and in (with) favor

WORD CHECK

Put a ✔ next to the Hebrew word that means the same as the English.

.1	memory	☐ אַהֲבָה
		☑ זִכָּרוֹן
.2	and in (with) favor	☑ וּבְרָצוֹן
		☐ וְרָצָה
.3	memory	☑ זֵכֶר
		☐ מִצְרָיִם
.4	sanctification	☑ קָדוֹשׁ
		☐ בָּרוּךְ
.5	work of creation	☐ נֵר שֶׁל שַׁבָּת
		☑ מַעֲשֵׂה בְּרֵאשִׁית
.6	in (with) love	☑ בְּאַהֲבָה
		☐ בְּרֵאשִׁית
.7	going out from Egypt	☐ לְעוֹלָם וָעֶד
		☑ יְצִיאַת מִצְרָיִם

87

WORD CHECK

Direct student to complete the exercise individually. Have them cover the Prayer Dictionary. Then ask them to uncover the Prayer Dictionary to self-check.

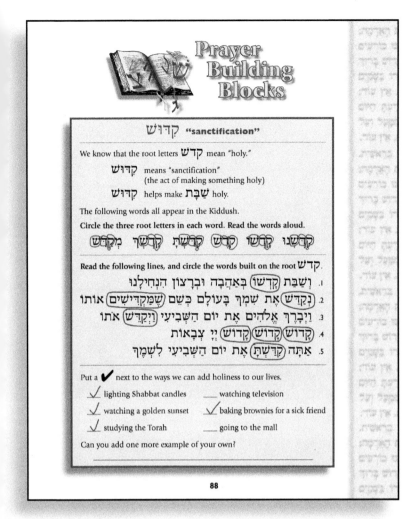

PRAYER BUILDING BLOCKS
קָדוֹשׁ "sanctification"

- Read and complete the first part of the page together. Ask students to follow the directions and circle the root letters ק ד שׁ in the six words at the bottom of the first part.

- Then ask students individually to read these six words aloud twice. Ask which reading was students' "personal best."

- Direct students to page 86 and ask them to find the six words in the קָדוֹשׁ which are based on the root ק ד שׁ and lightly circle them (*last word, line 2; fifth word, line 3; second word, line 5; second and sixth words, line 6, and sixth word, line 7*)

- Form reading partners by counting off 1-2, 1-2, 1-2 . . . Ask each partnership to practice reading each complete sentence in the קָדוֹשׁ on page 86 that contains a word built on the root ק ד שׁ. Then, ask each partnership to read a sentence aloud to the class, either individually or together.

- Using the same reading partnerships, direct the class back to page 88, lines 1–5 in the middle of the page. Ask students to circle all the words built on the root ק ד שׁ. Have the reading partners practice reading the first line aloud with Partner 1 reading all but the circled words, and Partner 2 interrupting to read the circled words as they occur. Then, for the second line, the two partners switch and alternate for each of the following lines.

The Fruit of the Tree
Add the new words built on ק ד שׁ to the tree with the root ק ד שׁ.

Adding Holiness

Allow students time to place check marks at the bottom of the page next to the ways we can add holiness to our lives, and to add a personal example at the conclusion of the activity. Then, have students connect the actions they checked and the example they wrote to a specific Jewish value. (*lighting Shabbat candles: it is a blessing of mitzvah; watching a golden sunset: shows the appreciation for our world that we also show by praising God in a blessing; studying Torah: refer to "An Ethical Echo" on page 38 of the textbook—it is said that* Talmud Torah *is the most important mitzvah of all; baking brownies and taking them to a sick friend is the mitzvah of* בִּקוּר חוֹלִים—*visiting the sick*)

IMAGINE THAT!

Read the paragraph aloud with students. Explain that our tradition also teaches us that Shabbat is to be greeted like a queen when it arrives.

THINK ABOUT THIS!

Encourage students to share their ideas and insights. *(being holy: living according to Torah; following the commandments to help our fellow human beings and to preserve the earth; acknowledging God's presence through prayer; being a witness—עֵד—to God's presence in the world in the way we lead our lives; continuing Jewish traditions)*

PRAYER BUILDING BLOCKS
זִכָּרוֹן, זֵכֶר "memory," "remembrance"

Read and complete this section with students.

"Leaving Home"

Explain to the class the difference between זִכָּרוֹן and זֵכֶר. *(זִכָּרוֹן refers to a tangible remembrance; זֵכֶר refers to an intangible remembrance—a memory)*

Ask students to imagine that they must leave their homes, perhaps permanently. Tell them to list five tangible objects they would take with them as a זִכָּרוֹן and five memories they would take as a זֵכֶר. Have them share their lists. *(tangible: favorite stuffed animal, photos; memories: good friends, happy times at play)*

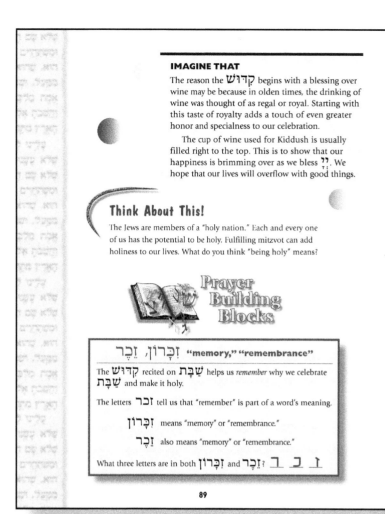

IMAGINE THAT

The reason the קִדּוּשׁ begins with a blessing over wine may be because in olden times, the drinking of wine was thought of as regal or royal. Starting with this taste of royalty adds a touch of even greater honor and specialness to our celebration.

The cup of wine used for Kiddush is usually filled right to the top. This is to show that our happiness is brimming over as we bless יְיָ. We hope that our lives will overflow with good things.

Think About This!

The Jews are members of a "holy nation." Each and every one of us has the potential to be holy. Fulfilling mitzvot can add holiness to our lives. What do you think "being holy" means?

Prayer Building Blocks

זִכָּרוֹן, זֵכֶר "memory," "remembrance"

The קִדּוּשׁ recited on שַׁבָּת helps us *remember* why we celebrate שַׁבָּת and make it holy.

The letters זכר tell us that "remember" is part of a word's meaning.

זִכָּרוֹן means "memory" or "remembrance."

זֵכֶר also means "memory" or "remembrance."

What three letters are in both זִכָּרוֹן and זֵכֶר? ז כ ר

89

The קִדּוּשׁ helps us remember events in our history that are reasons for joy. One reason for joy is mentioned in these words from the קִדּוּשׁ.

זִכָּרוֹן לְמַעֲשֵׂה בְרֵאשִׁית

remembrance of the work of creation

Circle the Hebrew word that means "memory" or "remembrance."

....

Another reason for joy is found in the following words from the קִדּוּשׁ prayer.

זֵכֶר לִיצִיאַת מִצְרָיִם

memory of the going out from Egypt

Circle the Hebrew word that means "memory" or "remembrance."

....

Which three letters tell us that "remember" is part of a word's meaning?

ר כ ז

Read the following sentences and circle the words built on the root זכר.

1. וַיֹּאמֶר מֹשֶׁה אֶל הָעָם, זָכוֹר אֶת הַיּוֹם הַזֶּה.

2. בָּרוּךְ אַתָּה, יְיָ אֱלֹהֵינוּ, מֶלֶךְ הָעוֹלָם, זוֹכֵר הַבְּרִית, וְנֶאֱמָן בִּבְרִיתוֹ וְקַיָּם בְּמַאֲמָרוֹ.

3. מְקַדֵּשׁ יִשְׂרָאֵל וְיוֹם הַזִּכָּרוֹן.

4. לְמַעַן תִּזְכְּרוּ וַעֲשִׂיתֶם אֶת כָּל מִצְוֹתַי, וִהְיִיתֶם קְדֹשִׁים לֵאלֹהֵיכֶם.

5. וּזְכַרְתֶּם אֶת כָּל מִצְוֹת יְיָ וַעֲשִׂיתֶם אֹתָם.

90

Reviewing Reading Skills

Complete the first two parts of the page together. Practice reading the following two complete sentences in the קִדּוּשׁ on page 86:

1. line 2 through line 4 (fourth word)

2. line 4 (fifth word) through line 5 (fifth word).

Then direct the students to lines 1–5 on the second half of page 90.

- Ask them to circle all the words built on the root ז כ ר and read the words aloud.

- Then, ask each student to write the circled words clearly on individual slips of paper and place the slips in a "memory box."

- Lastly, ask individual students to select a word at random from the memory box and read aloud the complete line that contains the word. Repeat so that all students have an opportunity to select and read.

The Fruit of the Tree

Create a new fruit tree with three roots. Write the root letters ז כ ר on the three roots—one letter on each root. Write the meaning ("remember") on the trunk of the tree. Create fruit for the tree, one piece of fruit for each word built on the root.

THE HOLIDAY CONNECTION

You may wish to mention the many wars the modern State of Israel has fought to gain and maintain its independence as a Jewish nation. Bring a map to class so students can see how small Israel is compared with its neighboring countries. Why is it important to have a day to remember those who died in Israel's wars? (*honors their memory; honors their valor; gives comfort to their families; shows appreciation for the lives given so that the Jewish people can have their own country; encourages heroism in the future*)

Ask students to answer the question on page 91 individually. Call on them to share their responses. (*we remember how the Jewish people gained independence through war and the sacrifice of lives; we do not take independence for granted*)

Extending the Discussion

The Jewish people honor the memory of our loved ones and our ancestors in many ways. We honor them with rituals: *yahrzeit*; Yizkor; High Holiday memory books. We honor them with holidays: Yom Ha'atzmaut; Passover; Yom Hashoah. And we even honor them with food: the salt water in which we dip the green karpas at the Passover seder reminds us of the tears of the slaves in Egypt.

THE HOLIDAY CONNECTION

There is a special day in the Jewish year when we remember all the brave soldiers who died in Israel's wars. We call this day יוֹם הַזִּכָּרוֹן, the Day of Remembrance. יוֹם הַזִּכָּרוֹן is observed in Israel on the day before יוֹם הָעַצְמָאוּת, Israel's Independence Day.

Why do you think the solemn יוֹם הַזִּכָּרוֹן is observed one day before the joyous Day of Independence?

_____

_____

_____

91

Photo Op

- Discuss the symbols on the decorative flags. The six-pointed star is a symbol of the Jewish people. What is the Hebrew term? (מָגֵן דָּוִד)

- The seven-branch menorah surrounded by olive branches is Israel's state emblem. Torah Note: The seven-branch menorah is first described in the Torah (Exodus 25:31–37).

- What is the symbolism of the olive branch? (*peace*) Torah Note: In Parashat Noah a dove returns to the ark with an olive branch. The waters had receded. Peace had returned to the earth (Genesis 8:10–11).

- What celebration is depicted in the photo? (יוֹם הָעַצְמָאוּת) If any of your students have been in Israel on יוֹם הָעַצְמָאוּת or participated in community-wide events, ask them to share their experiences with the class.

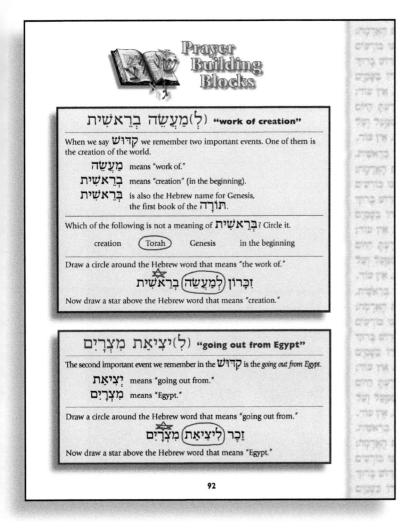

PRAYER BUILDING BLOCKS

(לְ)מַעֲשֵׂה בְרֵאשִׁית "work of creation"

Read the first part of the page aloud with students. Direct them to complete the section individually. Then review their answers. Challenge students to read the complete sentence in the קָדוֹשׁ that contains the (לְ)מַעֲשֵׂה בְרֵאשִׁית prayer building block (*page 86: line 2 through the fourth word, line 4*).

Extending the Lesson

Teach students the Hebrew names of the five books of the Torah. The Hebrew name is taken from the first important word in each book.

Genesis	בְּרֵאשִׁית
Exodus	שְׁמוֹת
Leviticus	וַיִּקְרָא
Numbers	בְּמִדְבָּר
Deuteronomy	דְּבָרִים

(לְ)יְצִיאַת מִצְרַיִם "going out from Egypt"

Read the second part of the page aloud with students. Direct them to complete the section individually. Then review their answers.

Challenge students to read the complete sentence in the קָדוֹשׁ that contains the (לְ)יְצִיאַת מִצְרַיִם prayer building block (*page 86: fifth word of line 4 through the fifth word of line 5*).

From the Torah

We read about the going out from Egypt in the second book of the Torah—*Exodus*, שְׁמוֹת (meaning "names"). It begins: "And these are the names of the sons of Israel who came to Egypt with Jacob, each coming with his household" (Exodus 1:1).

Review Questions

Why do we remember creation in the קָדוֹשׁ?

Why do we remember going out from Egypt in the קָדוֹשׁ?

INTRODUCING THE CONCEPT

Together with the students read the following portions of the קִדּוּשׁ and their English translations on page 86:

- "In God's love and favor...work of creation" *(sixth word of line 3 through fourth word of line 4)*

- "You chose us . . . sacred inheritance" *(sixth word of line 5 through second word of line 7)*

Explain: God chose the Jewish people for a unique destiny when, with love and favor, God gave us Torah and we accepted it. We were chosen to be a holy people living our lives according to the mitzvot in the Torah. "You shall be holy for I, Adonai your God, am holy" (Leviticus 19:2). Along with the gift of Torah comes the responsibility to honor and love God and Torah in return.

Discuss with students privileges they have and the responsibilities that go along with those privileges. You might focus on teams or organizations they belong to, and the responsibilities they have as members. Ask them why a responsibility is just as important as an honor, a privilege, or a membership. *(responsibilities indicate meaningful contributions to the group; when others count on you, you are a full-fledged member of the group)*

בְּאַהֲבָה "in (with) love"

Read and complete the first part of the page aloud with students. Ask students to highlight or circle the prayer building block בְּאַהֲבָה, which appears twice in the קִדּוּשׁ on page 86 *(lines 3 and 6)*. Circle the English meaning.

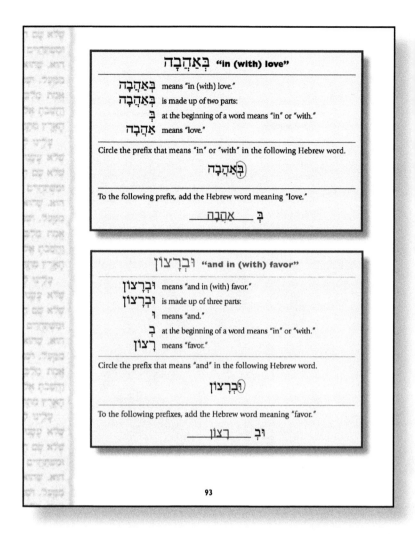

וּבְרָצוֹן "and in (with) favor"

Read and complete the bottom part of the page aloud with students. Have students highlight or circle the prayer building block וּבְרָצוֹן, which appears twice in the קִדּוּשׁ on page 86 *(lines 3 and 7)*. Circle the English meaning.

Form two-person reading partnerships. Direct reading partners to practice reading the sentences that contain these phrases from page 86: first word in line 2 through fourth word in line 4; sixth word in line 5 through second word in line 7. Then have the students read the final sentence in the קִדּוּשׁ together (בָּרוּךְ . . . הַשַּׁבָּת).

DID YOU KNOW?

The leader of the service recites the קִדּוּשׁ at the end of Friday evening services and we say the קִדּוּשׁ at home before our Shabbat meal.

Why is the קִדּוּשׁ said *twice* on a Friday evening?

The custom of saying the קִדּוּשׁ both at home and in the synagogue began almost 2,000 years ago. Travelers who were far from their homes were often fed and sheltered in the synagogue. To ensure that these people heard the קִדּוּשׁ, the leader of the service recited it in the synagogue for all to hear.

One glass of wine in the synagogue allows all the people there to fulfill the mitzvah of saying the קִדּוּשׁ.

94

DID YOU KNOW?

Ask students to read this section silently. After they are finished, ask (sample questions):

- Where are the two places that we recite קִדּוּשׁ on Friday evening? *(synagogue and home)*

- Would it be true to say the synagogue was a place of refuge for travelers? Explain. *(yes, travelers found food and shelter in the synagogue)*

Reading Practice

Read the blessing over wine and the קִדּוּשׁ on page 86 in unison with students. Call on individuals to read one line each.

Form the class into groups of seven by counting off: 1-2-3-4-5-6-7; etc. Within each group, ask each member to select one of the seven sentences beginning with the blessing over wine, and ask the group members to practice their sentences in 1–7 order. Then, ask each group to read the complete קִדּוּשׁ to the class, with each group member reading his or her sentence in turn.

Singing the קִדּוּשׁ

Teach students the melody for chanting the blessing over wine and the קִדּוּשׁ.

Extending the Opportunity

Create an opportunity for the class to chant קִדּוּשׁ into a tape recorder so that they may hear themselves sing it.

FLUENT READING

Challenge students to find and read words built on the following roots. Have students read the word and the complete line. א ה ב—line 3; ב ר כ —line 9; מ ל כ—line 7; ז כ ר —lines 2, 9; ק ד ש—lines 2, 5, 7.

Reviewing Roots: A Fruit Salad

Remove all the fruit from the root trees of previous lessons and mix them in a salad bowl to create a "fruit salad." Have students sort out the fruit according to the root and place each one back on the correct tree. Ask each student hanging a piece of fruit to read the word before placing the fruit on the tree.

Nine Innings

Create two baseball teams. Allow the students to pick team names. Ask each player on each team to select one of the nine lines on page 95 to read. (If there are fewer than nine players, then players will need to be responsible for more than one line.) The rules:

- Batting Practice: Ask players to practice reading their line(s) with their teammates.

- Game Time: Each line is the inning of a baseball game. The teams earn a "home run" by reading the line correctly. Players on each team alternate reading the lines to complete the game.

- Rain Delay: If a player makes a mistake in reading, he or she can play one more time in order to score. But if the line is not read correctly the second time, the team does not score and the next team goes.

WORKSHEET

Duplicate and hand out Worksheet 9 to review concepts in the קִדּוּשׁ.

FLUENT READING

Practice reading the lines below.

1. וַיְכֻלּוּ הַשָּׁמַיִם וְהָאָרֶץ וְכָל צְבָאָם.

2. וַיְבָרֶךְ אֱלֹהִים אֶת יוֹם הַשְּׁבִיעִי וַיְקַדֵּשׁ אֹתוֹ.

3. וּמֵבִיא גוֹאֵל לִבְנֵי בְנֵיהֶם, לְמַעַן שְׁמוֹ, בְּאַהֲבָה.

4. עֲבָדִים הָיִינוּ לְפַרְעֹה בְּמִצְרָיִם.

5. אַתָּה קִדַּשְׁתָּ אֶת יוֹם הַשְּׁבִיעִי לִשְׁמֶךָ.

6. לִבְנֵי יִשְׂרָאֵל עַם קְרֹבוֹ, הַלְלוּיָהּ!

7. זָכוֹר אֶת יוֹם הַשַּׁבָּת לְקַדְּשׁוֹ.

8. אִלּוּ הוֹצִיאָנוּ מִמִּצְרַיִם וְלֹא קָרַע לָנוּ אֶת הַיָּם–דַּיֵּנוּ!

9. בָּרוּךְ אַתָּה, יְיָ אֱלֹהֵינוּ, מֶלֶךְ הָעוֹלָם, אֲשֶׁר בָּחַר בָּנוּ מִכָּל הָעַמִּים וְנָתַן לָנוּ אֶת תּוֹרָתוֹ.

95

FAMILY EDUCATION

Ask the class to continue to develop the Shabbat Handbook to be used at a Family Shabbat Dinner (see Family Education in Lesson 7). Add the קִדּוּשׁ after the blessing over wine. Along with the Hebrew include the English translation and decide if you want to include transliteration. Draw on class discussions as students decide on an explanation of the significant themes in the קִדּוּשׁ.

Add final touches to the handbook such as drawings or illustrations. Consider including the song Shalom Aleichem; the traditional family blessing Birkat Hamishpaḥah, which is recited by parents over their children; and the blessing after the meal—Birkat Hamazon (see textbook page 59).

Develop a family page for students to write the names of family members. Include blessings that students write for their parents. Invite families to a class family Shabbat dinner and Friday evening services. Each family will use the family Shabbat Handbook to welcome Shabbat.

Duplicate and send home with students the Family Education page "As a Family: Remembering Creation and Freedom" (at the back of this guide) to create an "at home" dialogue reflecting the major themes of the קִדּוּשׁ.

Name: _____

קָדוֹשׁ

1. What is the meaning of the word קָדוֹשׁ?
   _____

2. The Jewish people are a "holy people." In your own words explain what it means to be a "holy people."
   _____

   _____

3. Why do we introduce the קָדוֹשׁ with the blessing over wine?
   _____

   _____

4. What is the root for the word קָדוֹשׁ? _____ What is its English meaning?
   _____

5. Write the number of the root next to its English meaning.

_____ love	מ ל כ	.1
_____ bless, praise	ב ר כ	.2
_____ remember	צ ו ה	.3
_____ faith	א ה ב	.4
_____ rule	א מ נ	.5
_____ evening	ע ר ב	.6
_____ command	ז כ ר	.7

6. Write the English meaning for each phrase highlighting the themes of the קָדוֹשׁ:

   2. זֵכֶר לִיצִיאַת מִצְרָיִם   1. זִכָּרוֹן לְמַעֲשֵׂה בְּרֵאשִׁית

   _____   _____

   How is each theme connected to Shabbat?

III. ENRICHMENT AND SUPPLEMENTARY MATERIALS

FAMILY EDUCATION

As a Family

Name: _____

Coming Together in Community

בָּרְכוּ אֶת יְיָ הַמְבֹרָךְ.

Barechu et Adonai hamevorach.

Praise Adonai, who is to be praised.

בָּרוּךְ יְיָ הַמְבֹרָךְ לְעוֹלָם וָעֶד.

Baruch Adonai hamevorach l'olam va'ed.

Praised is Adonai, who is to be praised forever and ever.

_____

In class we have been studying the Barechu (בָּרְכוּ) prayer. This prayer calls the community together for worship. It requires a *minyan*—a group of at least ten adults—in order to pray.

This sense of community reminds each one of us that we are not alone. It also reminds us that others in our community need our support and friendship. And it provides an opportunity for us to share our joyous occasions with others, as well as a place for us to receive support and comfort from our friends and neighbors when we are sad or troubled.

As a family, think about reasons the Jewish community comes together, each one of us for the others. And think about why you, as a family, come together with your Jewish community. Please share your thoughts with us on this page; your child will then share them with the class.

_____

_____

_____

_____

_____

_____

_____

HINENI—THE NEW HEBREW THROUGH PRAYER 1 © Behrman House Publishers
www.behrmanhouse.com/family

Evening and Morning

בָּרוּךְ אַתָּה, יְיָ אֱלֹהֵינוּ, מֶלֶךְ הָעוֹלָם,

אֲשֶׁר בִּדְבָרוֹ מַעֲרִיב עֲרָבִים...

Baruch Atah, Adonai Eloheinu, Melech haolam, asher bidvaro ma'ariv aravim.

Praised are You, Adonai our God, Ruler of the world,
whose word brings on the evening.

This prayer is said during the evening service, as daytime turns into evening and the stars appear in the sky.

בָּרוּךְ אַתָּה, יְיָ אֱלֹהֵינוּ, מֶלֶךְ הָעוֹלָם, יוֹצֵר אוֹר...

וּבוֹרֵא אֶת הַכֹּל.

Baruch Atah, Adonai Eloheinu, Melech ha'olam, yotzer or . . .
uvorei et ha'kol.

Praised are You, Adonai our God, Ruler of the world, who forms light . . .
and creates all things.

This prayer is said during the morning service, as we look forward to the day.

In each prayer, we praise God for the cycle of time, for giving us the day, for bringing us to a restful end of day and evening, and then again the next morning for restoring us after a night's rest.

What are the favorite times of day for each of the members of your family? Is it morning? twilight? the darkness of night? Why is this time special? What has God created that you treasure most?

_____

_____

_____

_____

Preparation for Name Day

Send home a personal invitation from each child inviting parents to class for a special Name Day. Prior to sending home the invitations, ask each student to tell you his or her Hebrew name. For students who do not have Hebrew names, arrange a meeting in person or on the telephone with the families and the rabbi so that the families can select names.

On Name Day: יוֹם שֵׁם

Hand out the page "As a Family: Name Day." Share with the assembled families parts of the discussions you held in class about a "good name." Then read and discuss with them the prayer and the introductory statement on the "As a Family" page. Encourage families to talk among themselves, especially with their children, about how they selected their child's name. Perhaps it was the meaning of the name that held significance for them. If the child was named for someone, encourage family members to talk about that person.

Name Cards: שֵׁם Cards

Have a selection of Hebrew name books on hand so that each family can look for the spelling of the child's Hebrew name and its meaning. (As an alternative, you can create a class name dictionary with the Hebrew names of all the students and their meanings prior to the program.)

Ask families to create personal שֵׁם cards. On the provided card (see below) ask family members to print the child's Hebrew name and its meaning, and also to create an artistic representation of the meaning of the name on the card.

Materials Required

Pre-cut oaktag for the name cards; Hebrew letter stencils or press-on letters; felt-tip markers, calligraphy pens, and pencils; crayons, paints, and glitter; magazines with pictures; scissors, glue, and paint brushes.

Concluding Ceremony

After the cards are made, invite the families to join together in reciting the שְׁמַע. Call on students to explain how the second sentence is recited in a quiet voice and why it is recited this way.

Display the name cards so that families can view all the designs.

Note: You can send home the "As a Family: Name Day" sheet if you do not hold a Name Day.

Name: _____

Name Day

שְׁמַע יִשְׂרָאֵל: יְיָ אֱלֹהֵינוּ יְיָ אֶחָד.

Shema Yisrael: Adonai Eloheinu Adonai eḥad.

Hear O Israel: Adonai is our God, Adonai is One.

———————————

בָּרוּךְ שֵׁם כְּבוֹד מַלְכוּתוֹ לְעוֹלָם וָעֶד

Baruch shem k'vod malchuto l'olam va'ed.

Blessed is the name of God's glorious kingdom forever and ever.

Through prayer, word, and deed, Judaism teaches us to glorify God's name and God's world.

———————————

Each of us through our words and our deeds brings honor to our own name, and to the name of our family. The Hebrew names we are given honor our Judaism, just as they honor our past and our present. The Hebrew names we give our children are symbolic of a new generation which continues the Jewish way of life, and they honor our families and our ancestors.

As a family, think about the Hebrew name you gave your child and discuss it together.

- How was the name selected?

  _____

- If your child was named for someone, who was that person, and what would you like to share with your child about that person?

  _____

- If your child was given a name with a special meaning, what is that meaning, and what would you like to share about it?

  _____

- How do we each bring honor to our names?

  _____

Name: _____

Showing Love

וְאָהַבְתָּ אֵת יְיָ אֱלֹהֶיךָ
בְּכָל־לְבָבְךָ וּבְכָל־נַפְשְׁךָ וּבְכָל־מְאֹדֶךָ.

Ve'ahavta et Adonai Elohecha
b'chol-l'vavcha uv'chol-naf'sh'cha uv'chol-m'odecha.

You shall love Adonai, your God,
with all your heart, and with all your soul, and with all your might.

———————————————

Our tradition teaches us of God's great love for humanity, and that the gift of the Torah at Mount Sinai was a demonstration of this love. The prayer above—the Ve'ahavta—teaches us to respond with love of our own.

And so it is with families as well. Parents show their love for their children, and children, in turn, demonstrate love for their parents.

How do the members in your family show love for one another?

_____

_____

How do members in your family demonstrate love for God and appreciation for the gifts of life?

_____

_____

In what ways does the love in your home remind you of the words of the Ve'ahavta?

_____

_____

As a Family

Name: _____

Crossing the Sea

מִי-כָמֹכָה בָּאֵלִם, יְיָ?

Mi chamochah ba'eilim, Adonai?

Who is like You among the gods, Adonai?

מִי כָּמֹכָה, נֶאְדָּר בַּקֹּדֶשׁ

Mi kamochah, nedar bakodesh

Who is like You, majestic in holiness

נוֹרָא תְהִלֹת, עֹשֵׂה פֶלֶא?

Nora t'hilot, oseh feleh?

Awesome in splendor, doing wonders?

_____

This song is found in the Torah (Exodus 15:11).

The Israelites sang these words as they crossed the Sea of Reeds from slavery in Egypt to freedom. The lives of the Jewish people were changed completely and forever by the Exodus from Egypt.

Today, too, we cross from one stage in our lives to another. Sometimes we move to a new house or even a new city, at other times we start a new school, or we add to our family. And at other times our lives change because of sadness and loss.

Please share on this page some of the important crossings in the life of your family, and how those crossings changed each of the members of your family.

_____

_____

_____

_____

_____

Name: _____

Sharing Blessings

בָּרוּךְ אַתָּה, יְיָ אֱלֹהֵינוּ, מֶלֶךְ הָעוֹלָם...

Baruch Atah, Adonai Eloheinu, melech ha'olam . . .

Praised are You, Adonai our God, Ruler of the world . . .

_____

Our tradition teaches us not to take life for granted. Our prayers give thanks for the blessings in our lives. It is through our prayers and blessings that we say "thank you" to God, and that we recognize the importance of these things. Our traditional way of saying "thank you" is by reciting a blessing, a בְּרָכָה (*b'rachah*). Blessings each begin with the words at the top of this page.

Consider the things that are most important to your family. Write a family blessing, on behalf of all of you, for one of these things. Or, if you prefer, have each family member write a blessing for something that is personally important.

You can begin your blessing any way you choose.

_____

_____

_____

_____

_____

_____

_____

_____

_____

_____

Name: _____

Celebrating Shabbat

Each Friday night we welcome Shabbat in our homes. We place candles, wine, and two covered ḥallot on our Shabbat table. We light the candles and recite the blessing.

בָּרוּךְ אַתָּה, יְיָ אֱלֹהֵינוּ, מֶלֶךְ הָעוֹלָם, אֲשֶׁר קִדְּשָׁנוּ
בְּמִצְוֹתָיו וְצִוָּנוּ לְהַדְלִיק נֵר שֶׁל שַׁבָּת.

Baruch Atah, Adonai Eloheinu, Melech ha'olam, asher kid'shanu
b'mitzvotav v'tzivanu l'hadlik ner shel Shabbat.

Praised are You, Adonai our God, Ruler of the world, who makes us holy
with commandments and commands us to light the Sabbath light.

_____

We recite a blessing over wine and drink the wine.

בָּרוּךְ אַתָּה, יְיָ אֱלֹהֵינוּ, מֶלֶךְ הָעוֹלָם,
בּוֹרֵא פְּרִי הַגָּפֶן.

Baruch Atah, Adonai Eloheinu, Melech ha'olam,
borei p'ri hagafen.

Praised are You, Adonai our God, Ruler of the world,
who creates the fruit of the vine.

_____

We uncover the ḥallah, recite the blessing, and pass a piece of ḥallah to each person at the table.

בָּרוּךְ אַתָּה, יְיָ אֱלֹהֵינוּ, מֶלֶךְ הָעוֹלָם,
הַמּוֹצִיא לֶחֶם מִן הָאָרֶץ.

Baruch Atah, Adonai Eloheinu, Melech ha'olam,
hamotzi leḥem min ha'aretz.

Praised are You, Adonai our God, Ruler of the world,
who brings forth bread from the earth.

_____

The flames of the Shabbat candles cast a peaceful glow on our dinner table. What can each member of your family do to continue the glow throughout the week?

_____

_____

_____

_____

Name: _____

The Miracle of Ḥanukkah

בָּרוּךְ אַתָּה, יְיָ אֱלֹהֵינוּ, מֶלֶךְ הָעוֹלָם,
שֶׁעָשָׂה נִסִּים לַאֲבוֹתֵינוּ
בַּיָּמִים הָהֵם בַּזְּמַן הַזֶּה.

Baruch Atah, Adonai Eloheinu, Melech ha'olam,
she'asah nisim la'avoteinu
bayamim haheim baz'man hazeh.

Praised are You, Adonai our God, Ruler of the world,
who made miracles (did wondrous things) for our ancestors
long ago, at this season.

_____

On each of the eight nights of Ḥanukkah we recite this blessing after the blessing over the candles. We think back to the story of the oil that lasted for eight days. And we remember the miracle of a small band of people—the Maccabees—who fought for religious freedom, and won against all odds. We remember that after the Maccabees won their fight, they cleansed the Temple, and re-dedicated it to God. And we remember that the word Ḥanukkah means "dedication."

Imagine This!

As we recall the miracles, or wondrous things, our ancestors experienced long ago at this season, we also think about the wondrous things in our own families. Share these "miracles" with each other.

_____

_____

_____

_____

_____

_____

As a Family

Remembering Creation and Freedom

זֵכֶר לִיצִיאַת מִצְרָיִם   זִכָּרוֹן לְמַעֲשֵׂה בְרֵאשִׁית

Zeicher liy'tziy'at Mitzrayim   *Zikaron l'ma'aseih v'reishit*

memory of the going out from Egypt   memory of the work of Creation

---

When we recite the Kiddush, we remember the work of creation and we remember our going forth from Egypt—our Exodus from slavery to freedom. Only a free people can celebrate, worship, and rest. Only as a free people were we given the opportunity to receive Torah with its commandments to remember Shabbat (Exodus 20:8) and to observe Shabbat (Deuteronomy 5:12).

Think about ways your family can celebrate creation on Shabbat. What can you do to demonstrate your appreciation of nature? of other people? Please share your ideas with us.

_____

_____

_____

Our tradition teaches us that we were liberated from slavery so that we could serve God—so that we could observe God's laws of justice, peace, and compassion, and honor the holy days of our calendar. Think about ways your family can celebrate its freedom to be a part of the Jewish people. For example, how can attending Shabbat services or inviting guests to share a meal with you help you celebrate our people's freedom to fulfill the teachings of Torah?

_____

_____

_____

_____

TECHNIQUES FOR USE WITH SPECIAL NEEDS STUDENTS

Like most classes, yours probably includes a diverse group of students with different learning styles and needs, who achieve mastery at different rates. The variety of activities in *Hineni* offers your students a broad selection of learning opportunities that can be easily modified for students with special learning needs.

Without practice, students frequently lose some of their Hebrew decoding skills over the summer. This is particularly true of students with special learning needs. It is helpful to assess such students' decoding skill levels individually at the very beginning of the new school year and review the letters and vowels with them.

It is important to use a diagnostic-prescriptive approach. By noting students' decoding errors, you can identify their needs, reteach problematic letters and vowels, and provide the necessary practice to bring the students back up to speed. Use your school's primer to reteach basic reading skills. Retest the students to be certain that they have mastered the troublesome items.

Here are some teaching tips that can help you work more effectively with special needs students.

- Be ready to assist the students in decoding new words and phrases. Model the correct pronunciation and phrasing before they read any segment of the book. Do not let them struggle. Reinforce word attack skills by breaking words into syllables. Repeat words and phrases several times, and do not assume that all your students will be able to read them fluently and accurately when they see the same words and phrases again later.

- Students with significant learning difficulties may have trouble keeping up with the class. Prioritize your goals for them. Identify the core elements of the text that you want them to master; this will help them keep up with the rest of the class. Allow extra time for them to finish an assignment, or reduce the number of items they are expected to complete. Offer them other modes of responding, e.g., orally instead of in writing, underlining or circling instead of copying, or working together with an aide or a buddy.

- Although the Hebrew text in *Hineni* has separated and numbered lines, some students may benefit from using an index card or pencil to help track across the line. In some instances, masking the rest of the page to reduce distractions can enable them to read more easily.

- Some students, especially those who are shy, lack confidence, or have learning differences, are reluctant to read aloud in class. You can provide an alternative method of monitoring their reading progress by listening to small groups while the rest of the class is working on the other sections of the lesson. This is also a more efficient use of class time.

- For students who require additional support in order to achieve mastery, enlist parents as partners in the educational process. Short periods of daily practice with an audiotape at home will help the students retain what they have learned in class and build toward fluency and accuracy. Parents can "sign off" on the practice schedule even if they themselves do not feel that they are competent Hebrew readers.

By adapting your teaching techniques to meet the individual learning styles and special needs of your students, you can help every member of your class master the skills in this book.

ANSWERS TO
WORKSHEETS

Name: _____

בָּרְכוּ

1. Complete the בָּרְכוּ by adding the missing words. Select your words from the box.

בָּרְכוּ	בָּרוּךְ	וְהַמְבֹרָךְ	בָּרוּךְ

   _____ אֶת יְיָ _____

   _____ יְיָ הַמְבֹרָךְ לְעוֹלָם וָעֶד.

2. Write the root letters of the three missing words in the above exercise. ב ר כ

3. What is the meaning of this root? bless   praise

4. How many people are needed to form a מִנְיָן? 10
   How old must one be to be counted as part of a מִנְיָן? 13 years old for a boy;
   12 years old for a girl

5. How do you pronounce God's name: יְיָ, יהוה? Adonai

6. Explain in your own words the purpose of the בָּרְכוּ.
   to call the congregation together for the prayer service; it is
   a signal to begin the service

7. Why do we need a מִנְיָן to recite the בָּרְכוּ?
   (Hint: Think about the significance of a מִנְיָן. Think about the purpose of the בָּרְכוּ.)
   the מִנְיָן represents the community (the congregation); the
   בָּרְכוּ calls the community (the congregation) together for the
   prayer service

Name: _____

יוֹצֵר אוֹר / מַעֲרִיב עֲרָבִים

1. At what time of day do we recite מַעֲרִיב עֲרָבִים? evening
   creating twilight and darkness

2. For what do we praise God in מַעֲרִיב עֲרָבִים? every day

3. At what time of day do we recite יוֹצֵר אוֹר? morning
   creating morning light and giving

4. For what do we praise God in יוֹצֵר אוֹר? us renewed energy

5. What does the root ערב mean? evening

6. What does the word אוֹר mean? light

7. The blessings יוֹצֵר אוֹר and מַעֲרִיב עֲרָבִים speak of God's love for us.
   How is Torah a symbol of God's love? Torah tells how God created the
   world for us and gave us laws to live by, guides us, teaches us

8. Write the correct number next to the matching English phrase.

4	forms light	עֹשֶׂה שָׁלוֹם .1
1	makes peace	מַעֲרִיב עֲרָבִים .2
5	and creates all things	בּוֹרֵא חֹשֶׁךְ .3
2	brings on the evening	יוֹצֵר אוֹר .4
3	and creates darkness	הַבּוֹרֵא אֶת הַכֹּל .5

Name: _____

שְׁמַע

1. Write the words of the שְׁמַע in the correct order.

   שְׁמַע   יְיָ   אֱלֹהֵינוּ   אֶחָד   שְׁמַע   יְיָ

   שְׁמַע יִשְׂרָאֵל יְיָ אֱלֹהֵינוּ יְיָ אֶחָד

   Unscramble the phrases to write the English meaning of the שְׁמַע prayer.

   Hear O Israel   Adonai is One   Adonai is our God

   Hear O Israel Adonai is our God Adonai is One.

2. In the Torah, the last letter in the first word and in the last word of the שְׁמַע are larger than the other letters.

   שְׁמַע   אֶחָד

   What is the English meaning of the word עֵד? __witness__

3. Why is the word עֵד so important in understanding the meaning of the שְׁמַע?

   We are a witness that God is One when we say the שְׁמַע

4. Who is יִשְׂרָאֵל? __the Jewish people:__ עַם יִשְׂרָאֵל

   What is יִשְׂרָאֵל? __the Jewish state:__ אֶרֶץ יִשְׂרָאֵל

5. Write the words of the second sentence of the שְׁמַע in the correct order.

   בָּרוּךְ   שֵׁם   כָּבוֹד   מַלְכוּתוֹ   לְעוֹלָם   וָעֶד

   בָּרוּךְ שֵׁם כְּבוֹד מַלְכוּתוֹ לְעוֹלָם וָעֶד

   Unscramble the phrases to write the English meaning of the second sentence.

   of God's glorious kingdom   forever and ever   blessed is the name

   Blessed is the name of God's glorious kingdom forever and ever

---

Name: _____

וְאָהַבְתָּ

1. Circle the correct word: The וְאָהַבְתָּ comes before/(after) the שְׁמַע.

2. Unscramble the English letters and write the word below the matching root.

   vole   eneingv   leur   slebs

   בָּ רַ ךְ   עָ רַ ב   אָ הַ ב   מָ לַ ךְ

   bless   evening   love   rule

3. Circle the part of the word that means "you" or "your." וְאָהַבְ(תָּ)

4. The מְזוּזָה:

   Where do we place a מְזוּזָה? __on the doorposts of our house__

   What passages from Torah are inside a מְזוּזָה? שְׁמַע וְאָהַבְתָּ

   What does a מְזוּזָה represent? __our love for God, respect for God's commandments, a Jewish home__

5. How has God shown love for us? __gave us Torah; chose us to represent God's teachings__

6. How do we show our love for God? __reflect God's teachings in the ways we choose to live, the choices we make, the respect we show for God's name and Torah__

   Why are we to teach the words of Torah to our children in each generation? __to keep our heritage alive; each generation will renew its relationship with God; each generation will understand God's teachings__

Name: _____

שִׁירָה בַּיָּם

1. When did the Jews first sing שִׁירָה בַּיָּם? **When they saw the parting of the Sea of Reeds and safely crossed to freedom after the Exodus from Egypt**

2. Why did they sing this song? **To praise God and give thanks for their freedom**

3. Which book of the Torah contains this song? **Book of Exodus**

4. Number the three lines to place the שִׁירָה בַּיָּם prayer in the correct order. Then number the English to match the Hebrew.

2 Who is like You, majestic in holiness — מִי כָמֹכָה נֶאְדָּר בַּקֹּדֶשׁ **3**

1 Who is like You among the gods, (other nations worship), Adonai — מִי כָמֹכָה בָּאֵלִים יְיָ **2**

3 Awesome in splendor, doing wonders — יְיָ, נֶאְדָּר ... **1**

5. According to a legend, how did the Maccabees get their name? **When Judah, leader of the Jewish soldiers, called the Jews to battle, he called out יי מִי כָמֹכָה בָּאֵלִים יְיָ. The first letters of these words spell מַכַּבִּי.**

6. Draw a line to match each root with its meaning.

rule — ק ד שׁ

holy — א ה ב

bless, praise — מ ל ך

love — ב ר ך

7. Write the correct root below each word.

בְּמִצְוֹתָיו   קִדְּשָׁנוּ   וְצִוָּנוּ   יְיָ   קָדוֹשׁ

אֱלֹהֵינוּ   אַתָּה   בָּרוּךְ   נֵר   קֹדֶשׁ

Name: _____

בְּרָכוֹת

1. Number the first six words of a בְּרָכָה in the correct order.

מֶלֶךְ **5**   יְיָ **3**   הָעוֹלָם **6**

אֱלֹהֵינוּ **4**   בָּרוּךְ **1**   אַתָּה **2**

Number the additional four words that are recited in בִּרְכַּת שֶׁל הַמִּצְוָה in the correct order.

קִדְּשָׁנוּ **2**   אֲשֶׁר **1**   וְצִוָּנוּ **4**   בְּמִצְוֹתָיו **3**

2. What three Hebrew letters tell us "holy" is part of a word's meaning? ק ד שׁ

Circle these three letters in the word קִדְּשָׁנוּ.

What two Hebrew letters tell us "command" is part of a word's meaning? צ ו

Circle these two letters in the words בְּמִצְוֹתָיו וְצִוָּנוּ.

3. Write the number of the Hebrew word next to its English meaning.

3 Adonai — בָּרוּךְ .1

5 ruler — אַתָּה .2

2 you — יְיָ .3

6 the world, the universe — אֱלֹהֵינוּ .4

1 praised, blessed — מֶלֶךְ .5

4 our God — הָעוֹלָם .6

9 with (God's) commandments — אֲשֶׁר .7

7 who — קִדְּשָׁנוּ .8

10 and commands us — בְּמִצְוֹתָיו .9

8 makes us holy — וְצִוָּנוּ .10

בְּרָכוֹת שֶׁל שַׁבָּת

1. Unscramble the ending for each blessing we recite to welcome Shabbat. Then complete the English meaning of each blessing.

Candlelighting:

אֲשֶׁר קִדְּשָׁנוּ בְּמִצְוֹתָיו   בָּרוּךְ אַתָּה יְיָ אֱלֹהֵינוּ מֶלֶךְ הָעוֹלָם
וְצִוָּנוּ / שֶׁל / לְהַדְלִיק / נֵר / שַׁבָּת / בְּמִצְוֹתָיו

Praised are You, Adonai our God, Ruler of the world ___who makes us holy with___
___commandments and commands us to light the Sabbath light (candle)___.

Wine:

בּוֹרֵא פְּרִי הַגָּפֶן.   בָּרוּךְ אַתָּה יְיָ אֱלֹהֵינוּ מֶלֶךְ הָעוֹלָם
הַגָּפֶן / פְּרִי / בּוֹרֵא.

Praised are You, Adonai our God, Ruler of the world ___who creates the fruit of the vine.___

Bread:

הַמּוֹצִיא לֶחֶם מִן הָאָרֶץ.   בָּרוּךְ אַתָּה יְיָ אֱלֹהֵינוּ מֶלֶךְ הָעוֹלָם
הָאָרֶץ / מִן / הַמּוֹצִיא / לֶחֶם

Praised are You, Adonai our God, Ruler of the world ___who brings forth bread from___
___the earth.___

2. Which of the three בְּרָכוֹת is a זְכוֹר שֶׁל בְּרָכָה? ___candlelighting___

3. Explain the symbolism of each ritual.

Candlelighting: ___Reminder of the two mitzvot: "Remember" and "Observe" Shabbat___

Wine: ___Symbol of joy and abundance of our blessings___

Bread: ___Represents all the food on the table; double portion of manna the Jews collected___
___in the desert on the sixth day (2 hallot)___

הַבְדָּלָה

1. Unscramble the ending for each blessing we recite in the הַבְדָּלָה ceremony. Then complete the English meaning of each blessing.

Wine:

בּוֹרֵא פְּרִי הַגָּפֶן.   בָּרוּךְ אַתָּה יְיָ אֱלֹהֵינוּ מֶלֶךְ הָעוֹלָם
הַגָּפֶן / בּוֹרֵא / פְּרִי

Praised are You, Adonai our God, Ruler of the world ___who creates the fruit of___
___the vine.___

Spices:

בּוֹרֵא מִינֵי בְשָׂמִים.   בָּרוּךְ אַתָּה יְיָ אֱלֹהֵינוּ מֶלֶךְ הָעוֹלָם
בּוֹרֵא / בְשָׂמִים / מִינֵי

Praised are You, Adonai our God, Ruler of the world ___who creates the varieties___
___of spice.___

Havdalah Candle:

בּוֹרֵא מְאוֹרֵי הָאֵשׁ.   בָּרוּךְ אַתָּה יְיָ אֱלֹהֵינוּ מֶלֶךְ הָעוֹלָם
הָאֵשׁ / בּוֹרֵא / מְאוֹרֵי

Praised are You, Adonai our God, Ruler of the world ___who creates the fiery lights.___

2. What is the meaning of the word בּוֹרֵא in each blessing?
___who creates___

2. When does the הַבְדָּלָה ceremony take place? ___At the conclusion of Shabbat when there___
___are three stars in the Saturday night sky___

3. What does the word הַבְדָּלָה mean? ___separation___

4. Explain the significance of the הַבְדָּלָה ceremony. ___To separate the uniqueness___
___of Shabbat from the rest of the week___

LESSON 8
Worksheet

Name: _____

בְּרָכוֹת שֶׁל יוֹם טוֹב

1. Write the English next to each Hebrew word.

miracles	נִסִּים .4	matzah; unleavened bread	מַצָּה .1		
tree	עֵץ .5	shofar; ram's horn	שׁוֹפָר .2		
fruit	פְּרִי .6	the earth	הָאֲדָמָה .3		

2. The following phrases are blessing endings. Write the Hebrew name of the holiday next to the matching blessing ending.

סֻכּוֹת   פֶּסַח   חֲנֻכָּה   שַׁבָּת   רֹאשׁ הַשָּׁנָה

פֶּסַח   1. עַל אֲכִילַת מַצָּה

רֹאשׁ הַשָּׁנָה   2. לִשְׁמֹעַ קוֹל שׁוֹפָר

סֻכּוֹת   3. לֵישֵׁב בַּסֻּכָּה

חֲנֻכָּה   4. שֶׁעָשָׂה נִסִּים לַאֲבוֹתֵינוּ
בַּיָּמִים הָהֵם בַּזְּמַן הַזֶּה

פֶּסַח   5. עַל אֲכִילַת מָרוֹר

שַׁבָּת   6. אֲשֶׁר קִדְּשָׁנוּ בְּמִצְוֹתָיו

סֻכּוֹת   7. עַל נְטִילַת לוּלָב

3. Describe the miracles to explain the blessing ending:
שֶׁעָשָׂה נִסִּים לַאֲבוֹתֵינוּ בַּיָּמִים הָהֵם בַּזְּמַן הַזֶּה

menorah oil in Temple burned for 8 days when there was only

enough oil for 1 day; victory for religious freedom; small army

(Maccabees) defeated a mighty army (Greek Syrians)

LESSON 9
Worksheet

Name: _____

קִדּוּשׁ

1. What is the meaning of the word קִדּוּשׁ? __sanctification__

2. The Jewish people are a "holy people." In your own words explain what it means to be a "holy people."

__have a special relationship with God; chosen by God to receive the Torah__

__and observe mitzvot; have a responsibility to follow teachings of Torah__

3. Why do we introduce the קִדּוּשׁ with the blessing over wine?

__wine represents royalty and we praise God, our Ruler; wine represents__

__joy and symbolizes the joy of creation and freedom__

4. What is the root for the word קִדּוּשׁ? __קדשׁ__ What is its English meaning? __holy__

5. Write the number of the root next to its English meaning.

__4__ love	ק ל ל .1
__2__ bless, praise	ב ר ך .2
__7__ remember	א ה ב .3
__5__ faith	א מ ן .4
__1__ rule	מ ל ך .5
__6__ evening	ע ר ב .6
__3__ command	ז כ ר .7

6. Write the English meaning for each phrase highlighting the themes of the קִדּוּשׁ:

1. זִכָּרוֹן לְמַעֲשֵׂה בְרֵאשִׁית
__remembrance of the work of creation__

2. זֵכֶר לִיצִיאַת מִצְרַיִם
__memory of the going out from Egypt__

How is each theme connected to Shabbat?

1. __God rested on the seventh day following the work of creation__

2. __Only a free people can rest from work, can come together as a community to praise God__